Life Is
Goodbye

Life Is
Hello

Life is Goodbye. Life is change. Life means having and holding—then letting go and giving up—even what we love the best.

Life is also Hello. We can survive loss. We can move beyond endurance to accept new and different joys into our lives.

Discover the art of possibility. The tools are your own creativity and faith. You have it all within you. You can do what you need to do to be healed...

This pain won't last forever.

Life Is Goodbye

Life Is Hello

Grieving Well Through All Kinds of Loss

Alla Renée Bozarth, Ph.D.

HAZELDEN

Hazelden
Center City, Minnesota 55012-0176

©1982, 1986 by Alla Renée Bozarth, Ph.D.
All rights reserved. First edition 1982. Second edition 1986
Previously published 1982 by CompCare Publishers
First published by Hazelden Foundation 1994
Printed in the United States of America
No portion of this publication may be reproduced in any
manner without the written permission of the publisher

ISBN: 1-56838-057-7

To Pesha, Mary, Sally, and Barbara —
   witnesses and spiritual midwives,
   who helped me to die and give rebirth
   to myself through the long labors
   of grieving.

Acknowledgments

Author's poems first published in other books

From *Gynergy*, Alla Bozarth-Campbell, Wisdom House Press, 1978
  "Syzygy"
  "Limenality"

From *Sparrow Songs*, René Bozarth and Alla Bozarth-Campbell, St. Paul's Press and Wisdom House Press, 1982
  "Parting"
  "Visiting the Old Folks' Home"
  "Aging"
  "Recovery: Dissociation of Sensibility"
  "Life Does"
  "Love Mantra for Letting Go"
  "Birth Is a Movable Feast"
  "Dance for Me When I Die"

From *In the Name of the Bee & the Bear & the Butterfly*, Alla Bozarth-Campbell, Wisdom House Press, 1978.
  "Freedom"
  "In the Name of the Bee & the Bear & the Butterfly"

Book jacket design by Susan Hancock Rinek
Jacket photograph by Judy Minter
Drawings by The Illustrators, Costa Mesa, California

Contents

One: Attitudes about Grieving 1

Cultural Influences:
"Thou Shalt Not Fall Apart" 2
Stoicism and the Jackie Kennedy Syndrome . . 3
Anti-process and the Silver Lining Syndrome 5
Anti-feeling in a Stressful Society 7
Ritual: Help or Hindrance 9
Countercultural Influences:
"Primal Scream or Bust" 15
The Middle Way: "Two, Four, Six, Eight —
Integrate, Integrate, Integrate" 17
A New Law: Each Thing in Its Own Time 18
Redeeming the Process:
Falling Apart and Coming Together 18
The Validity of Control 20
Bravado vs. Courage to Grieve 21

Two: Grief: Loss of Part of One's Self 23

Grievous Loss: Being Cut Off from
Someone or Something That Represents
a Part of One's Self 24
Self-image and Self-definition 26
Reconciliation to Loss; Redefining One's Self ... 27

Three: Grieving: How It Feels, What It Does,
  What You Can Do about It   31

How It Feels   31
  Shock   31
  Feelings Emerge: Confusion   33
  Four Feeling Stages: Fear, Guilt,
    Rage, Sadness   35
  Primary and Secondary Feelings   40

What It Does   41
  Physical Symptoms   41
  Emotional Symptoms   43
  Intellectual Symptoms   44
  Spiritual Symptoms   44
  Behavioral Symptoms   45
  Change in Attitude   46
  The Danger of Implosion   46

What You Can Do about It   49
  Expressing Grief and Taking Care
    of Yourself: Some Practical Suggestions . . .   50

Four: Four Styles of Grieving   75

The Hero   77
The Martyr   80
The Crazyperson   83
The Fool   85

Five: Life Is Goodbye/Life Is Hello   89

Death in Grief: Disintegration   90
  The Pain   90
  The Bleeding   91

Rebirth Out of Grief: Reintegration   92
     The Dance.   92
     The Healing   93

Six: Death   99

Loss of a Link with Life 100
Loss of Intimacy. 106
Death of a Dream 109
Political Grief 110
Collective Grief 111
Death is Being Left. 111
A Note on the Communion of Saints. 113

Seven: Birth and Parenting. .121

Loss of Physical Self-image in Pregnancy 122
Loss of Freedom and Privacy. 123
Loss of Self-confidence 124
Loss of Security in Childbirth 124
Loss of Physical Union 126
Other Losses in Parenting. .127

Eight: Change 131

Change in Place 132
Change in Position. 134
Change in Person. 135
Change in Consciousness .137
Children and Change 138
Chemical Dependency and Change. 142

Nine: Separation.................................149

    Parting: Separation 149
    Divorce: Dissolution 153
    Physical Separation and Spiritual Alienation 155
    Instances of Alienation: Violation 156
    Grievous Alienation from God 157
    Grievous Alienation from Self 158

Ten: Sickness 161

    Self-image and Sickness 162
    Illness of a Loved One 164
    A New Idea of Wholeness 166

Eleven: Success.................................171

    Loss of the Struggle or Loss of Ambition........172
    Sacrificing Failure...........................173
    The High Cost of Winning...................174

Twelve: Essentials of the Art of Grieving..........175

    Another Kind of Grieving 178
    Creativity in the Face of Reality 180
    Feeling One's Feelings 180
    Healing Wounds...........................182
    Reconciliation 183

Epilogue..189
About the Author 221
Appendix: Helpful Resources...................223

Author's Introduction

This book comes to you from my experience as one who has gone on a grief journey several times. One time, to be sure, took me further than I believed one could go. But each time, including the last, I came back. I came back to life. I came back to myself, to my work, to my loved ones. Though I do not share the details of those personal journeys except for their lessons and gifts, or occasionally as one story in the context of many co-travelers' stories, I come to you in this book on the basis of what I have learned personally in my soul about letting go.

Because I came back when I believed absolutely that I never would, I offer you testimony that it *is* possible to be broken by loss and to be healed. Because I am deeply grateful for those who sustained me in my brokenness, I want to pass on what they gave to me.

At a certain point in my last grief journey, I knew that I could not continue alone. I needed the security and protection of someone who could witness my process, as I allowed a part of myself to die. I also knew that only when we allow ourselves to go all the way through any kind of death experience can we come out the other side into whatever life is beyond the abyss. I knew this theoretically, but part of the death was in relinquishing even this — even my faith in life itself. I knew this to be a necessary condition of my own healing, if healing were indeed to come. I told my therapist exactly what I wanted from her: "Be my witness. Testify in my behalf, to me, as to the validity of my experience. Witness the truth of my pain, of my loss. I know that I must die now, and in time I know that I will be reborn. But having said that, I now need to let go of that knowledge — to die, even in my faith. Be with me. Hold on to me. Don't let me go. Be an anchor in whose presence I can safely become lost at sea. Help me to find my way back." And she did — this, and more.

The gifts which I did not ask for came also. Though I am a priest and a therapist, it was only as a broken human being that I embarked on my grief journey. I knew that a therapist originally was an attendant who wrote down the message of the gods who spoke through the dreams of those hurt souls who went to the Temple to incubate — to receive a healing dream while sleeping in the sacred place. It was the vocation of the therapist to speak back and record the divine utterance to the dreamer upon receiving the message while the person spoke in sleep, or soon after waking, and this witnessing, repeating back, and recording had a mediating effect between ego and psyche, human and divine, and from this mediation, wounds in the soul were touched and healed.

I listened to my therapist with ears alert to what the gods might have to tell me from her deep, reverent, and respectful attendance on my hurt soul. She did not let me blame myself or others for reality: reality simply is. The most important thing that she did for me was to tell me over and over, "The pain won't last forever. It won't last forever." For six months I did not believe her. One aspect of deep grief is loss of the imagination. One cannot imagine a time when one is not in pain. Though I did not believe her words, I believed in her as a human being who had also suffered.

The witness to me of her own grieving gave me trust in her. When she told me of her devastation at her sister's sudden death at an early age, I knew that I could trust her. So for six months, I leaned on her faith to carry me. Only at the end of that time did I begin to notice that I was not the same shattered creature who had first walked into her room — I could function a little better than before. Most importantly, I could laugh once in a while. Perhaps I was changing. Perhaps she was right, and the pain wouldn't last forever in that consuming way! I began to believe again for myself. I had come through spiritual death and was at last on my way toward rebirth. The journey was long, but it did not take forever. It happened *in time.*

To be human and alive means to absorb loss on a daily basis. We are faced with losses, small or great, all along the way. Not all losses are grievous. Indeed, most of the small ones we hardly notice; they do not disconnect us from ourselves. But the larger, disconnecting losses — the grievous ones — provide our greatest opportunities to live more deeply, to learn more of the meaning of our own lives.

When the time comes for you to go through grievous loss, I wish these gifts for you: First, may someone who has known that road tell you, over and over, "This pain won't last forever." And second, when you hear these words, may you have the gift of trust. I cannot give you that gift of trust, but I *can* say the words for you, "This pain won't last forever." And in time your own experience will restore the trust.

Then you, too, can pass on the first gift.

Good-Bye Means
God Be With You

Last words heard
clenched in the muscles,
held against grief
worked in the bone;
life pulls away
from the grey-eyed child.

Last words spoken
still harm, now
worked down
the remaining gaps
in the body, through
follicles, each Goodbye
of a lifetime pressed
in a strand
for the grey-haired child.

Grey is a passage
through which life can flow.
"God-be-with-you"
"God-be-with-you"
Hold on.
"God-be-with-you"
"God-be-with-you"
Let go.

One

Attitudes about Grieving

Grieving is a normal, healthy, healing activity. Grieving is an experience that we all encounter sooner or later as part of the human condition on this planet. Grieving is something that human beings must do in order to survive losses.

Grieving is hard. It need not be hellish.

What often makes grieving hellish are all the messages we get about it — especially the messages that tell us that sad feelings, expressed or unexpressed, are inappropriate, awkward, and often selfish.

Where do the messages about grief come from? What influences our conscious and unconscious attitudes about grieving?

I believe that the strongest influences are important cultural attitudes against the expression of feelings and the value of painstaking process. These attitudes are communicated to us in blatant and subtle ways — often in our families, in school, in the marketplace.

An opposite point of view — much more limited in its influence — comes out of some of the "pop" psychologies, with their emphasis on the theatrics of self-expresion, whether related to genuine feeling or not.

Then there are the influences of more moderate psychologies, which call upon us to become "integrated" or "whole" persons, an expectation which may seem unrealistic in the face of intense grief.

After a brief examination of these influences which add to unwritten laws against honest grieving, we can consider an alternative, a new unspoken permission allowing the feeling activity of authentic grief. We can learn to "grieve well."

Cultural Influences: "Thou Shalt Not Fall Apart"

Certainly not *all* feelings are looked on as bad or disgraceful. The message is that "good" feelings of happiness and well-being ought to be expressed. People should behave in a way that makes everyone else around them feel comfortable.

Telephone commercials on television always show people calling their loved ones long distance to express some happy feeling to them across the miles. This is well and good. But what is not shown is that people also need to reach across the miles to one another for love and support in times of emotional pain and crisis. No one ever falls apart seriously in the ideal world of the TV commercial. Why? Because it's unpleasant to see someone in emotional pain. Emotional pain, unlike physical pain, is not acceptable in our culture. Unlike the seemingly acceptable violence of television, it makes the viewer feel responsible and guilty in some vague, discomfiting way.

Grief is taboo.

Stoicism and the Jackie Kennedy Syndrome

The strongest communication of the grief-is-taboo idea in our culture came to American families through their television sets in the early sixties. We all watched the impressive funeral proceedings for John F. Kennedy. Days earlier we were struck with the horror of President Kennedy's assassination, the immediate anguished response of Jackie Kennedy, her pink suit splattered with blood, crawling over the back of the car, shrieking for help. What a striking and disconcerting contrast the funeral rite was — subdued, in order, according to form. Even the widow's tears were subject to public protocol. Behind her thin black veil we saw that same face, not contorted in pain, but mask-like, frozen, still. No human emotion intruded from Jackie's countenance into the controlled arena of grief-according-to-regulation.

I was disturbed by the self-restraint in Jackie Kennedy's bearing, by the way she had managed to bring her emotions under such severe control in so short a time. Now, years later, I see that what was disturbing about the experience for me was that her image at the funeral, walking stiffly beside her dead husband's cortège, was being put across to the American people as *an example of how we ought to behave in grief.* To be fair, she may have been in shock, but this was not the general interpretation of her behavior. I remember being puzzled by British commentators' reactions during a BBC interview. One of them called her "Queen Jackie" because of the "majesty" of her public bearing. Another praised her because she never let herself be seen with a tear or grimace on her face. To equate the apparent smothering of feelings with royal style seemed to me a marked instance of inhumanity. What human queen would not feel profound pain at the loss of a loved one? And why should she not show her pain and her love openly, assuring us of her humanity and our own? I have no doubt that my first image of Jackie Kennedy, wailing her despair spontaneously at the moment of disaster, was the truer of the two images given to the world.

Three hundred years before Christ, the Greek philosopher Zeno founded the school of Stoicism, which taught that all events were pre-ordained by divine will, and therefore human passions, joy as well as grief, were superfluous and should be avoided. The contemporary version of Stoicism leaves out the first part of this belief system and creates a caricaturized distortion of the original Stoics' ideals. Their ideal of serenity was based on trust and was far from the artificial calm of suppressed emotions that modern people so often suffer. Stoicism had as its goal the abolition of suffering. Modern social form merely denies it and so makes it worse, and more damaging to the sufferer. Instead of truly entrusting ourselves and our pain to a benevolent and all-wise God, we too often ignore the pain and cultivate emotional dishonesty as a virtue.

Anti-process and the Silver Lining Syndrome

Pain has a stubborn habit of not going away just because we deny it exists. In fact, the more pain is denied, the deeper it tends to go inside our bodies and souls, and the harder it is to identify and deal with and ultimately grow beyond.

Pain is an essential part of any growth process — the process of growing up, growing old, growing beyond grief. However, in our fast-paced world we have come to expect fast results. We expect to find the cloud with the silver lining without having to spend time looking for it. We have become impatient of processes.

How easy it is to avoid the real issue of suffering by looking immediately for ways to "grow" because of it. How many times have I sabotaged myself by leaping ahead of my own healing process, trying so desperately to "feel better" that I make myself feel even worse because I have added to my primary pain the new complication of failure! In cheating myself of the necessary time to feel bad I have cheated myself of the only process that could really heal me.

Ultimately, the only way to get through something is to get *through* it — not over, under, or around it, but all the way through it. And it has to take as long as it takes.

A bad situation is often just that, a bad situation, with nothing — at least at the time — to redeem it. The

Christian Good Friday is good only in retrospect. At the time it happened it was only bad. Horrible Friday. The end of the line. And if it had been less bad and horrible, Easter would not mean so much.

To pretend that real distress and real despair never happen is also to reject the possibility for redemption. Only what is really lost can be redeemed. Only what is truly dead can be brought back to life.

In the long run, pain that is met head-on is always assimilated, but only if we truly meet it and take it for what it is.

People fool themselves in many ways. We give ourselves false comfort when we by-pass the genuine sorrow of a deep loss or disappointment and tell ourselves some cheerful platitude. We lie to ourselves about our real feelings because it is sometimes easier to live a comforting lie than to work hard at the truth.

People with religious backgrounds may dismiss the pain of a situation with a shrug and a forced smile and say, "Oh well. It's God's will." God never wills pain, though pain truly faced may lead to untapped sources of grace. The important emphasis is on *truly facing* the total reality of the situation — the outer circumstances and one's full inner responses to it.

Those who have gone before us on their own grief journeys can reassure us that the needed strength is already there, within ourselves. Others who care about us can help us find access to it, so we can allow ourselves to take the time we need to go all the way through our own grief process.

Comfort and hope are words we often hear associated with grief.

The word "comfort" comes from two Latin words meaning "with strength." To be comforted truly is to be given the strength to meet a situation, to face it fully.

Hope is precious, but it does not wipe out pain. Pain becomes bearable when we are able to trust that it won't last forever, not when we pretend that it doesn't exist. We may be able to paint the clouds silver, but our dreams will show them more starkly grey than ever; dreams tell only the truth and can be tormenting if we deny the truth when we are awake.

A kind psychiatrist once told a friend of mine who was struggling to find something "good" in a bad situation, "A scar is really a scar, and it's no good trying to make it into a beauty mark." Scars may have their own value, and in time some of them may become transformed into beauty marks on their own. Some remain deformities as a reminder of the human condition we all share in pain and imperfection; some make us stronger than before, because scar tissue is very tough; some add a mystery of distinction to us which can either distance others or draw them to us; and some scars have no particular value at all.

Whatever the transforming nature of wounds which become scars in time, they are part of what makes each of us unique. We can learn to bear them with dignity as signs of what life has taught us, for we carry their meaning and lessons with us all our lives.

Anti-feeling in a Stressful Society

We all know what stress is: the feeling of being alternately or simultaneously closed in and pulled apart by the pressures and tensions of daily life. When life includes an experience of painful loss, stress sometimes becomes nearly unbearable.

Healthy ways to deal with stress involve recognizing our feeling responses to the bad situation which is causing the stress, and expressing those responses in safe ways.

The fine art of expressing feelings creatively is seldom learned at home or in school, and each generation grows up with a backlog of unexpressed feelings, or worse yet, feelings which sometimes are expressed in destructive, anti-social behavior.

In the adult world, men and women are given messages that "emotionalism" in response to deep personal grief has no place in their business or professional lives. As there continues to be professional pressure to "stifle yourself" (Archie Bunker's prescription to combat Edith's expressiveness) — or at least to leave emotions at home — working men and women become victims of frozen feelings in their personal lives as well.

The burden to suppress emotions and to function solely by reason is heaviest upon men — and upon women who are succeeding in traditionally male jobs. Even when their lives are falling to pieces, career persons are expected to preserve their on-the-job image of being totally together. Dedication to the company or the craft is expected to conquer any tendency toward self-indulgence in private grief. The effects can be devastating! Those who deny themselves necessary grieving time merely put off the process, which often emerges years later in the form of neurosis, or even psychosis.

Ritual: Help or Hindrance

One evening as I was celebrating the Eucharist — the sacrament of Holy Communion — with a small group of people in the large upper room of Wisdom House, a simple but startling thing happened. Someone had brought a small loaf of bread with a very hard crust for the Host. Usually we use matzos, which break easily. At the time in the liturgy for the breaking of the bread, I couldn't break the bread at all. I had to tear it apart, vigorously. Everyone present was focused on the action. The smooth surface of the loaf was crushed in the difficult, awkward process of tearing, pulling, and severing the bread from itself.

When it was done, we looked at one another. I was shaking, and I could see stunned recognition in the eyes of the others. So this was the meaning behind the words we hear every week: "This is my Body given for you." Not an easy gift, not a neat, elegant break, but a long, labored, untidy tearing of the flesh of the bread. The immaculate movement of the ritual had been powerfully interrupted by the stark messiness of reality — and this, after all, was the true meaning of what we were doing. Unbearable. Overpowering. Too much. All of us wanted to run away from the too-intense reality that had broken through the ritual we had grown so coolly accustomed to.

Shortly after that I read a paper on ritual by Roy Rappaport (see Helpful Resources, "Ritual," page 201). One of his insights made me recall that extraordinary moment in our worship experience. Rappaport pointed out that human beings ritualize events in order to limit

9

realities that are too much to bear — to contain them in formal patterns to make them bearable. We would risk being overwhelmed by the full impact of meaning and feeling in many life events if we had no way to harness and narrow them to fit our small and fragile capacity. (I am reminded of the words of T.S. Eliot in his *Four Quartets:* "Humankind cannot bear very much reality.") We can only bear the holy mysteries by limiting them in words and actions, and these become the rituals that make them safe. If we were not protected, we would be like the man in the Old Testament who touched the Ark of the Covenant with his bare hand and died.

All powerful human experiences have accompanying rituals, though we may not think of them as such. Rituals are patterns of expected actions or words. Laughter is the ritual of humor; trembling is the ritual of fear or excitement; tears are the ritual of sorrow; and hugging or kissing, the ritual of spontaneous affection. Without laughter, trembling, tears, or touching, we would be overwhelmed by the too powerful energies of humor, fear, excitement, sorrow, and affection. We would have no means of releasing our responses to these feelings, and our bodies could not contain them without discomfort or even damage. Each of us knows how bad it feels to have to suppress tears or laughter, to hide our natural trembling, or to hold back the strong desire to touch another person. There are times when to act on these urges would be inappropriate. But if we had to suppress them all the time, we would be hurting and harming ourselves unbearably.

We have cultural as well as religious rituals that enable us to respond collectively to the major events of life: birth, puberty, marriage, and death. We celebrate these events in formal ways which often include a religious ceremony, the offering of gifts, the gathering and sharing of food, and endless exchanges and talking about the fact and meaning of the event. These rituals provide release and an opportunity to express what needs to be expressed among the persons involved. Without them, communities would feel as bottled up and unsatisfied as the individual who is deprived of the opportunity to respond in instinctive ways to a moving situation.

Formal rituals which arise naturally from the spontaneous responses of people to events have a double function. They allow for a release of the overflow of human feeling, and they contain and limit the power of the event being commemorated so that it does not elicit too much feeling, or threaten the health of persons by overwhelming them or exploding them with too much energy.

Some formal rituals fail to rise up out of human reality and become painfully, repressively disconnected with human feeling. Such rituals are those which we experience as being "empty." They may indeed serve half the function intended by ritual. They may limit the full impact of the event being commemorated, but they may limit it too much, so that rather than protecting us from the dangerous extremes of feeling, they leave us cold, with no feeling response at all. Such rituals are worse than no rituals. We come away from them feeling pent up and maybe even miserable, because we expected to find a release and relief from the welling up inside us of feeling responses, and instead those feelings were pushed back down.

Funerals are the rituals we create to help us face the reality of death, to give us a way of expressing our response to that reality with other persons, and to protect us from the full impact of the meaning of death for ourselves. Some funerals fulfill these functions beautifully. Others fail. One funeral I attended was full of the music that the dead person had loved in life. In perfect counterpoint to the music came the rhythms of his loving aunt's sobbing, the outpouring of her heart in the midst of family and friends who could share her sorrow. It was perfectly appropriate to the reality of life and loss experienced by that community of people. At another funeral, there was no deviation from the words in the book, and no opportunity for personal expression of feeling. Everything was mechanical. Friends and family of the dead person created their own feeling-full rituals afterwards as they talked and ate together, sharing memories of their loved one and spiritual as well as physical nourishment to sustain them through their common loss.

Coldness and doing things by rote are not the only factors in unsatisfying rituals. Artificiality can be just as devastating to the release of genuine feelings. At my own mother's funeral in a tiny Russian Orthodox church, I expected to have a channel for my sorrow. When I saw a stranger sobbing in the church before anyone else arrived, my own feelings closed up. She was a professional mourner — someone paid to cry at funerals in case no real mourners showed up! She was as much a ceremonial fixture in that church as organists might be in other churches. Somehow for me to let myself weep there would cheapen my mother's memory by putting my feelings for her on a level with this stranger's trumped-up display.

Still, funerals which are done well provide a great service to the bereaved. They sacramentalize death in a healing way, showing outwardly that loss is real and absence painful, and that life contains and gives meaning to death.

Physical death is not the only kind of painful loss requiring the healing powers of a ritual. As individuals face losses of all sorts, they need to discover ways for themselves to express their feeling responses and to protect themselves from being overwhelmed.

One of the great areas of need for ritual in our society is divorce. I would like to see the creation of a religious observance of divorce, a ceremony or sacrament of severance, just as there are now religious ceremonies for marriage. Divorce is such a reality in our society, yet outside the emotional trauma of the courtroom procedure, there is no public way in which the persons' supportive community can commemorate with them the reality of their loss — the death of the marriage relationship — and incorporate that loss into a positive wish for their separate futures.

My vision for such a service includes a formal goodbye to the marriage and its dreams. By the time two people reach the decision to divorce, the negative dynamics of the relationship are obvious. Too often these blot out the good memories. A positive goodbye ritual means reclaiming and redeeming what was good between two people, while letting go of what was destructive. One may keep the love and let go of the pain, thus "unhooking" one's partner and one's self from impossible expectations. Each person may have the opportunity to express sorrow and forgiveness for the failure of the marriage and to wish the other well. Most important of all, if they have children, both may affirm publicly their love for and commitment to their children. Even if one partner decides not to participate, the other family members and friends may use the occasion to express grief and to reaffirm their love and commitment to each other in the future. A service encompassing this last aspect already exists. It is called "A Service of Affirmation When Parents Are Separating," and it is published in pamphlet form by Forward Movement Publications, 412 Sycamore Street, Cincinnati, Ohio 45202. This excellent liturgy reads:

> We acknowledge that we are now unable to meet one another's need and preserve those vows of matrimony which we once solemnly undertook. We say this with regret for we had wished to cherish each other and to see our union endure. Now, it seems best that we set each other free.
>
> We further acknowledge that we are entitled to this relief of our vows only as we accept our basic responsibilities for you [our children] and each other.

The parents pledge to extend support to one another, and each one separately pledges to continue sharing responsibility for the care and education of the children.

I would like to see the prohibitions against the expression of sorrow disappear from our culture, so that rituals such as this can serve their function on an effective and meaningful plane in helping people face and be reconciled to the reality of loss.

Countercultural Influences: "Primal Scream or Bust"

One obvious result of an extremely suppressive culture is the emergence of an extremely expressive counterculture. Popular psychologies of the past decade reflect the movement away from a thinking or analytical approach to therapy and towards methods which acknowledge the psyche and deal with feelings. These modes may not be authentically intuitive, integrative, or holistic. Often in the hands of unskilled or ungifted therapists, faddish therapies become nothing more than emoting sessions. Instead of psychic synthesis or integration through self-expression, destructive forms of psychological anarchy or emotional mayhem may occur.

Primal therapy and Scream therapy often put tremendous pressure on individuals to produce the Ultimate Emotion and then to emote it. Told how bad holding feelings in can be for people, the person who submits to Primal or Scream therapy can fairly easily come up with the desired results and work up a powerful case of the screams or the sobs. The problem is that forcing feelings to well up and to push them out does very little long-range good if these aren't connected with the whole context of a person's life. Anyone who is exhibitionist enough can scream on command, but no one is guaranteed good psychological health because of that ability. Fake feelings, like empty rituals, can be worse than no feelings or no rituals at all. They often leave one with the feeling of "being had," being promised something wonderful and then being left with an emptiness or a slightly rancid taste in the mouth of the soul.

To rebel against emotional inhibitions, either external or internal, simply for the sake of rebellion may be fun for the moment, like making mud pies. But in real life mud dries and hardens and cakes on our hands and becomes very uncomfortable unless we let the rain wash it off in time. The activity of working in the soil, digging weeds and planting seeds, may not always be as much fun as mud-pie-making and may be somewhat harder and more frustrating. But the results of this kind of involvement will be longer-lasting and will have the bonus of providing nourishment for one's self and for others as well.

In a similar way, genuine grieving — digging, weeding, growing — is not only a healthy activity, it is a worthwhile and necessary process. Forced sorrow is no substitute for the real grief process that may include anger, fear, guilt, or any complex interweaving of spontaneous feelings. A person who has experienced loss will not benefit from forcing out feeling responses any more than from denying feelings altogether. What is needed to grieve well is to discover the nature of the losses and their meanings and the impact of the feelings within ourselves, and then to find appropriate ways of responding. There are no short cuts.

The Middle Way: "Two, Four, Six, Eight — Integrate, Integrate, Integrate"

Therapies more sophisticated than the Primal or Scream sort can create more sophisticated pressures. In the mainstream of humanistic psychology, perhaps the most pervasive concept is that of integration. The existential therapies encourage us subtly but steadily to integrate all of our experiences into a beautiful wholeness. There is no heavy push to express strong emotion, but there is a quiet, often guilt-producing expectation that we work to "become whole," to "be centered." Sometimes the underlying assumption is that any state other than wholeness, integration, or centeredness is, if not sinful, at least not so good.

Those of us who have read Eric Fromm or Abraham Maslow or Frederick Perls may unconsciously begin to judge ourselves in the light of successful self-actualization, or self-acceptance, or creative love, or other-directedness, or total communication. We may judge ourselves as failing miserably, and blame ourselves because we *should* be doing better since we know so much about it. Insight *should* be enough, just as love *should* be enough, but it isn't. We should be "integrating" those bad feelings, or "converting" our tendencies to deny reality and pain. We should be "open." With all these "shoulds" in our heads, we haven't got a chance.

There are times in life when each of us, no matter how mature and well, is frankly unglued. We need to find a way to integrate the real disintegration within us — in other words, to release ourselves from the moral expectations of psychological growth, and simply allow ourselves the clumsiness and awkwardness of being hurt and untogether.

A New Law: Each Thing in Its Own Time

The only comforting thing about being hurt and untogether is that it won't last forever.

Once when I was going through an excruciating grief process and had actually lost the ability to imagine I would ever feel better, the most important words I heard were *it won't last forever.* I didn't believe the words, but I trusted the person who kept saying them to me, and knowing that *she* believed them got me through.

Redeeming the Process: Falling Apart
and Coming Together

I have worked with persons coping with loss at intense levels of feeling and discovery through differing situations: divorce or other kinds of death in relationships; retirement grief; unemployment; the grief of poverty; of emotional, physical, or spiritual sterility; of aging; of pregnancy, birth; of crises in parenting; the grief of sickness; and even the odd grief for loss of healthy striving that comes with success.

I myself have had occasion to grieve over the loss of one thing or another for the past nine years. I want to share with you what I have learned about the human process of grieving from observation and from experience. I want to offer you the assurance that it is possible and necessary to allow oneself to fall apart in order to be able to come together and that no part of the process can be safely ignored.

Sometimes in my own experience I have wondered, "Will it ever end?" It seems that I am never without a loss to face, some little death I have to die in order to become reborn once again. But again and again? One wearies of so much growth! A little rest in between — that's all I ask. But no, in reality life continues to be cyclic, not a steady, dependable straight line in one direction. It is not cyclic in that we never get anywhere, but like the rest of nature, human life has its regular seasons which extend the length of a lifetime and are repeated over and over again. The encouraging part of this realization is that if I can survive winter, I will be rewarded with a proportionately spectacular spring. As Shelley wrote so truly, "If winter comes can spring be far behind?" Well, it can seem far, but it will follow eventually, and usually just as we think we've reached our limit for enduring the deprivation, misery, or just plain tedium of winter.

Lately I have been helped by a metaphor from science. Astronomers are speaking and writing a great deal these days about Black Holes in space — invisible spots of such astounding density that an entire star or solar system may be sucked into one and promptly annihilated by its incredible compression and pressure. A terrifying possibility. No one really knows how this happens, but to complete the theory, the White Hole has been postulated. We are asked to imagine the Black Hole as an unimaginably vast and dense pressure chamber that is funnel shaped, the point of entry being the wide end of the funnel. What destruction, condensation, or transformation goes on inside the funnel is impossible to account for. What is observable is that beings and systems literally disappear. At some point, however, in the highly concentrated, invisible power chamber, activity mounts at the narrow end of the funnel and — surprise! A whole new universe explodes out the small side! The White Hole — the small end of the funnel — is the birth canal for new creations in space. The processes by which things fall into Black Holes and are transformed and pushed out the other side through White Holes, turning up as new beings in new worlds, are unfathomed as yet. But scientists believe they happen. Just so, I believe that within human experience there are spiritual counterparts to Black and White Holes.

Only by recognizing that we have somehow fallen into the annihilating space of a dense, high-powered Black Hole, and by experiencing the impact of it, can we hope eventually to be pushed out the other side into new life. This is a space-age metaphor for the age-old wisdom that only by losing yourself can you find yourself, only by dying can you be reborn.

The Validity of Control

I am not suggesting that one needs to "lose control" blindly in order to grieve well. Control is a very valuable trait. We learn self-control and control of the environment as very young children. The abilities to control ourselves and to manipulate our environment are absolutely necessary for survival and self-protection. Babies are helpless and dependent before they acquire these skills. Control becomes a problem or a barrier only when we fail to discriminate between situations in which we need to control our expressiveness and those in which to do so would not only be unnecessary, but harmful. Defenses are essential, but when we use them when they are not needed, they can hurt us.

There is a time in intense sorrow or rage when self-control can protect us from our own overwhelming feelings. And there is a time when we need to experience fully the feelings, to be controlled by them for a while, in order to become free of their destructive power in our lives and to incorporate them creatively into ourselves. In grief, there is a time when pain seems to be in control. Then there is a turning point and a time following when pain may still be there, but we are once again in charge of our lives.

Bravado vs. Courage to Grieve

To surrender to one's own grief and to become actively engaged in it require tremendous courage. This courage is vastly different from putting up a good front, showing a cheerful face to our friends when we are really hurting. That is mere pretense, hollow bravado, and serves no good purpose, for we seldom fool our friends any more than we fool ourselves.

Real courage is owning up to the fact that we face a terrifying task, admitting that we are appropriately frightened, identifying sources of help and strength outside and within ourselves, and then going ahead and doing what needs to be done.

Grief is a passion, something that happens to us, something to endure. People can be stricken with it, victims of it, stuck in it. Or they can meet it, get through it, and become quiet victors through the honest and courageous process of grieving. The difference between being grief-stricken and grieving is the difference between remaining a passive victim and actively making use of a situation. Grief is a passion to endure, but with the courage to grieve, you make it an action. Grieving is something you do. The following chapters will describe how to do it well.

Two

Grief: Loss of Part of One's Self

The dictionary defines *grief* as "an affliction of deep, acute sorrow; sadness and distress." The adjective form of the word, *grievous*, means something which is "hard to bear, causing physical suffering; severe; deplorable; atrocious." The archaic expression "to grieve someone" meant "to injure someone." To be grieved is to be injured.

All of the dictionary meanings of these related words suggest intense emotional suffering. The Latin words from which they derive are *gravare*, which means "to burden," and *gravis*, which means "heavy." To be grieved is to be heavily burdened, to bear something, to carry a weight.

These meanings cover a spectrum of intensity, from "hard to bear" to "atrocious." They also imply a movement from passivity to activity: from being injured or being burdened to bearing and carrying. There is nothing more helpless than being injured, nothing more assertive and purposeful than actively, willfully carrying something.

Grievous Loss: Being Cut Off from Someone or Something That Represents a Part of One's Self

What is it, exactly, that makes a loss hard to bear? And what determines the degree of intensity of our pain when we experience a loss? Why are some losses more painful than others when, to all appearances, they are minor and should be of little significance? Why do my friends fail to understand that this "little loss" affects me more deeply than some "bigger loss" I experienced with relative ease?

The answer to these puzzling questions lies in the personal meaning given to the object of loss, and how I feel about these relatively small material losses illustrates differences in meaning at deeper levels of loss. I may be very attached to some small possession — a favorite pendant — but when I lose it, I weep no tears and it is soon forgotten. Another article, a ring, may lie in my drawer unworn. But losing it hurts me for months on end. Why? Because my aesthetic attachment to the pendant was based on visual enjoyment and had no deep emotional significance to me beyond the pleasure of seeing and wearing it, while the less lovely ring was a gift from my grandmother. In some way I feel that it still links me to her spiritually. In losing it, I must create a new way of feeling close to my dead grandmother without the comforting physical object that had given me this meaning.

What to one person may be a grievous loss may amount to mere inconvenience for another. The key is in the meaning which a person invests in what has been given up or taken away by fate, circumstances, or will. In other words, the more someone or something means to me, the more of myself I have invested, given over, or entrusted outside of myself. In being cut off from that someone or something, I am in fact cut off from that part of me that the other represented. I have lost a part of my own self.

Finding my way back to the missing part of myself, reclaiming it from the person or thing now gone, is the process I have called grieving. It is, literally, a lifesaving process. Grieving is not only the way we survive a hurtful loss, but it is the way we can learn to live more creatively through and beyond the loss, into and out of a deeper part of ourselves. As I grow older I am discovering that survival is not enough in life; I want to honor the time of my life that I've been given by *living* it to the full. Life is a gift meant to be enjoyed, not just endured. Grieving is a way beyond endurance back to the enjoyment of this cherished gift, life.

Even in the face of grievous loss, there may be varying degrees of reaction. The greater the significance of the now lost person or thing, the more one is likely to believe "I can't be happy without . . ." or even "I can't feel whole without . . ." that other. In extremely painful loss — the kind which might indeed be "deplorable" or even "atrocious" to the sufferer — one may feel and actually believe "I can't live without . . ." All of

25

these statements really mean "I can't express a part of myself without . . ." The part of the self that is now stifled, buried, broken — *lost* — may be a small part of the total person, or an essential part. The degree to which the person feels lost to herself or himself measures the depth of the experience of grief through which the injured person must learn to live again.

Self-image and Self-definition

We all have a more or less accurate, more or less flexible image of ourselves. For most of us, this image is formed from the reflection of ourselves that we see in the eyes of our friends, loved ones, and daily associates. The more important a person is to us, the more seriously we take the image of ourselves reflected back to us from that person's eyes. In our earliest, most impressionable years, we learn a self-image that forms the basis, for good or ill, of the way we feel about ourselves throughout our lives.

As we grow, we modify this basic self-image by defining ourselves anew through new relationships as they develop, through our interaction with the environment, and through our own changing attitudes and behavior patterns. When there is a disruption in any of these — our relationships with others, our environment, or our own intrinsic behavior patterns and abilities — there is a corresponding disruption in our self-definition and self-image. Again, this change may be for good or ill. When it is for ill, usually some sense of loss accompanies the change. The disruption has a painful effect. Something grievous has interrupted our lives and shaken us, slightly or greatly, from our sureness about our selves. The very sense of self may be dimmed, dulled, or deadened.

Reconciliation to Loss; Redefining One's Self

Some kinds of loss make the task of redefining one's self quite clear. For instance, the loss of a spouse through death or divorce requires me to stop defining myself as a married person — a spouse — and to think of myself in the new image of single person. The loss of a job may force me to look at myself as someone other than a teacher, supervisor, builder, or whatever my work may have made me. Moving away from my home state may mean that I can no longer think of myself as a New Yorker, a Californian, a Minnesotan, or an Oregonian. Some familiar part of me may have to die in order for me to grow into whatever new definitions or images I take on in the normal course of life's changes.

This process of changing my way of seeing myself can be traumatic, particularly if it involves letting go of a special relationship or an ability I especially value in myself. A parent whose only child dies — experiencing perhaps the most devastating loss of all — must learn to let go of being a parent, or suffer the destructive consequences of empty longing and anguish or consuming envy when faced with images of happy parents and children. (Even if another child is born or adopted soon after, the parent must let go of the idea of parenting the particular child who was lost, or the new child will be

27

treated like the ghost of someone else.) In death, relationships change.

Believing in afterlife as I do, when my own mother died I came to experience her not so much as my mother, or myself as her daughter, but both of us as friends, or even sisters. The parent-child aspect of our relationship still remains, but I no longer focus on it as a *definition* of myself as a dependent person, or a person with a physically or emotionally dependent parent. A certain freeing or letting go is called for in the grieving process which may wrench the heart at the time, but which opens us outward to new possibilities for the self and for the self-in-relationship.

Another difficult change in self-definition is one that involves loss of a valuable personal gift, such as the loss of sight for an artist, or of hearing for a musician. How poignant is the familiar story of Beethoven, his hearing newly gone, who had to be turned around in order to see the audience's applause and outpouring of emotion in response to his Ninth Symphony!

An artist who not only earns a living through visual gifts but also finds personal worth in being able to see and create through perception faces tragic loss in blindness. Such loss is truly grievous, but need not be permanently devastating. The challenge is upon the artist to define herself or himself in new terms, perhaps by changing the material of art from visual to tactile by becoming a sculptor instead of a painter, or by becoming a teacher of art history. Or, instead of adapting to another form of art, this person may choose to give up art altogether and discover an entirely different way of life. Whatever the choice, the self-image of the person as an artist is bound to change, sometimes drastically.

It's no wonder, then, that a grievous loss — one that causes a person to lose access to a part of the self — can be disconcerting and distressing. It can even knock a person off her or his moorings, as if suddenly being cast at sea without knowledge of how to drop anchor. Being psychically at sea can be downright frightening. One may have to discover a whole new way to keep on being what one was — or how to become something else entirely.

Three

Grieving: How It Feels, What It Does, What You Can Do about It

This is the Hour of Lead —
Remembered, if outlived,
As Freezing persons, recollect the Snow —
First — Chill — then Stupor — then the letting go —

Emily Dickinson

How It Feels

Shock

A persons response to injury varies with the seriousness of the injury. The more severe the injury, the more pain or bleeding there will be. Some minor injuries — a pricked finger or a scraped knee — can be very painful for the moment, but the pain does not last long. In severe injury, the organism's defense is to go into shock.

Shock, in physical injury, is the body's way of protecting us against the reality of hurt, lest the pain of the hurt be too great to bear. Just as the body can numb itself, so can the human heart. When a pain is too sudden and too great, the heart goes numb. The numbness may last for a short or long time, depending on how long a person needs protection against the real pain of the hurt that has happened.

When we suffer a minor emotional injury, including one resulting from a loss, the pain may be very sharp but fast in subsiding, or the pain may be hardly noticed, depending on our general emotional health and constitution and on the circumstances. A greater injury or loss may cause deceptively little response: when a situation seems to deserve anguish, we may be puzzled to find that there is no feeling at all. This is emotional shock, a similar response to trauma that we know to be physically present following severe bodily injury.

Dr. Robert Jay Lifton, a Yale University psychiatrist, has observed a trait which he called "psychic numbing" in individuals who experienced sudden and violent loss through the nuclear holocaust of Hiroshima on August 6, 1945. These persons, and others whom he has interviewed since that time who have also experienced sudden and violent loss, seem to find protection from overwhelming emotion in an indefinite period of inability to absorb the reality of what has happened. It is as if the psyche has its own anesthesia in reserve, which it releases in times of overwhelming pain. The effects of this merciful function wear off as the individual gains the strength to accept and absorb reality, and the actual time frame varies from person to person and situation to situation.

Psychic numbing is likely to last longer in persons whose loss has been sudden and severe. Since their entire grieving process is likely to be of heightened intensity, the numbing may be of comparable degree. If an individual short-circuits mourning and remains in this numbed state as a permanent substitute for reality, there is an overdose of psychic anesthesia which may lead to a kind of psychic death. This condition need not be irreversible, but it may require sustained effort and outside help to reawaken the psyche from its slumber.

Feelings Emerge: Confusion

If the injury is indeed severe, affecting a deep part of the self, the pain might be so intense that the natural protection system of the emotional self first anesthetizes the sufferer, and then allows feelings to emerge only in a diffused way. The diffusion of feelings can be a way of de-fusing the potentially overwhelming and destructive capacities of such powerful emotions as rage and despair. It can also be a very confusing experience.

After a grievous loss I may feel so much nothingness that the only way I can describe it is to say:

> I feel empty
> I feel frozen
> I feel small, smaller and smaller
> I feel buried alive, put to sleep
> I feel dead
> I feel numb
> I feel nothing.

Slowly, as this natural anesthetic of the heart wears off, my metaphors may change:

> I feel myself under water, unable to move or breathe or see light
> I feel myself in a place with no top or bottom, a place with no walls and no protection
> I feel myself trapped in a burning room
> I feel myself shredded
> I feel myself on fire.

Where is the merciful numbness now? Such a cataclysm of feelings may occur that it will take constant effort to unravel and feel each one clearly. But there usually is an underlying pattern to the feelings.

When feelings first emerge, they may be muddled and overlapping, so that boundaries between different kinds of emotions dim or dissolve. This may lead to the panic which the early stage of shock prevented — a sense of getting nowhere, of flying faster and faster, of spinning in tight circles. A person may begin by feeling some clear sense of relief — perhaps that the long ordeal leading to this final loss is now over; and then an almost simultaneous resentment at having been put through the ordeal, followed by guilt — guilt at hundreds of haunting little irrational images of failure or malice, guilt at feeling relieved, guilt at feeling resentful. Then may come doubt and distrust — of oneself and others — anger, sadness, rage, despair, and finally the embarrassingly out of place giddiness that comes with complete fatigue.

All of these responses may crash in upon one's consciousness with a host of others. It is like being mad, glad, sad, and scared all at once. Confusion reigns. The degree of intensity and the particular appearance of any of these feelings depend entirely on the individual, and on the special circumstances and the nature of the loss. Each person has a unique emotional life, and a unique feeling pattern will emerge in grief, but many of these feelings are common to everyone who experiences loss.

Four Feeling Stages: Fear, Guilt, Rage, Sadness

It has been my observation and experience that there are four distinct stages in the grief process. I believe that most people find themselves in these feeling states while grieving well, and that usually, but not always, they come in this order: fear, guilt, rage, and sadness.

Fear sometimes prolongs the initial numbness one might feel, if a person is unskilled in self-expression or unused to dealing with feelings. Fear of my own feelings may cause me to repress them or deny them. Distrust of myself may give me the fear that my own actions will defeat me. This may be especially true if I'm afraid that my actions brought on the loss which has so hurt me. For example, I may have changed my career only to discover that in relocating I lost several important friendships which were part of my daily life before the move. If I am not yet sure that my choice was wise and my new position is not as happy as I had hoped it to be, I may fear to make such investments in the unknown in the future. Or perhaps I decided to risk expressing my anger to a friend who was not able to receive the care behind the anger, and I lost that relationship also. Or I planned an intervention to confront a relative with a drinking problem, and the person was unwilling to listen and eliminated me from his or her life.

If I risked expressing my feelings and then suffered loss, I may confuse this apparent cause and effect with my present situation and deprive myself of feeling my feelings in the present moment because it was feelings which got me here in the first place! If I believe my anger caused me to lose a friend, or my care caused me to lose a brother or sister, or my judgment took me from people I loved, I may fear to express anger, care, or judgment, even in dealing with my grief! Such a complex double bind is not uncommon, but it is unrealistic, and I need to talk through my situation with an objective person to restore my own perspective. I need my anger, care and judgment in order to cope with the painful loss I am experiencing. Whenever we take a risk, we need to know that our action may backfire or be ineffective, and we need to be willing to live courageously with that possibility.

When we sink into fear, we can become emotionally paralyzed. I may fear that others will ignore or betray me if I reveal my pain. I may withdraw like a turtle and never know that others are reaching out to me in care and concern. Or I may become openly hostile and aggressive to cover up my real fear of vulnerability and self-exposure. How often I have made the mistake, in refusing to let fear tyrannize me, of failing to let it serve me! If I am prejudiced against feeling, my fear of feeling will be strengthened, and I will become the victim of my own fear. Because I am so afraid of "losing control," I will stifle myself and isolate myself from others. I will not *lose* control; I have already lost it. Fear will be in control of me!

Respect your symptoms of fear as you respect a stop sign. They are nature's way of getting your attention. Take time, look, listen, evaluate, and act appropriately. Anxiety is unfocused fear. It usually warns you that you are avoiding your true feelings. Often in anxiety you fail to breathe properly, either by holding your breath or by hyperventilating. Slow down, and fully and gently receive and release each breath. As you inhale you may pray, "I am," and as you exhale, "in God's hands," for three deep, full breaths. To grieve well, you must breathe well. Simply attend — pay attention. When your breath is back, pray for strength to see and tune in to your true feelings. Respect yourself in your feelings.

There is another kind of fear that grips the human soul in times of crisis: *dread.* Dread is the deep anticipation of disaster, usually associated with a remembered horrible image. When a client of mine came in great distress after breaking off a relationship which she had truly wanted to end, I asked what her dominant feeling was. "Fear," she said. "I am afraid to be alone. I don't trust myself to keep myself safe. When I was three years old, my psychotic father set fire to our house when my mother was in church. Four of us little girls, all under five years old, called out to him. I saw him turn his back on us and walk out the door. Thank God my mother came home in time to take us to safety. I look like my father physically, and all my life I've been terrified that I, too, would walk out on people, turn my back on myself or others."

"That is true dread," I said. "Your experience was a deeply dreadful one, and you need to know that, and to allow yourself to feel the dread that belongs to that memory, that terrible reality of the three-year-old child. You then need to recognize that you have now found a way to triumph in your life — not just to survive, but to be all the way alive. Take courage from the rest of your history. You can learn again that you are trustworthy, that you are not your father, that you are motivated by compassion — as the compassion you feel for those children in the fire, yourself one of them. Your compassion will lead you into *response-ability*. You can take your own time, now, to teach yourself that you are trustworthy. You can also identify the 'guardian angels' in your life who have helped you, and who are there to help you now, to learn responsibility and loving care. You are free to reach out for help."

Guilt is connected with the self-doubt that often motivates fear. Whatever bad thing has happened to me, it must be *my fault.* "I did it wrong," or "I *should* have done it *this* way, or *another* way, or *not at all.*" "If only . . ." The Great Torture of *If.* Such thinking reinforces the feeling cycle of blame-and-shame. Shame is feeling bad about who one *is.* Guilt is feeling bad about what one *does.* Shame is the sense of having violated one's own ethical standards; guilt is the sense of having violated someone else's. Shame is introverted blame from oneself; guilt is introjected blame from outside oneself — what one perceives the judgment of others to be. These feelings may or may not be accurately connected with reality, and must be checked against reality and, if necessary, corrected. Otherwise one will either blame oneself or someone else.

The cycle can be broken and compassion restored only if I remove my thinking from the realm of blame-and-shame and am adult enough simply to acknowledge the reality of *what is*. If, after a long illness, my dependent relative has finally died and I am free from the burden of worry and care, I may very well feel *relief*. This does not mean that I am a bad person, or that I wished death to the person who has died. It simply means that a hard time is now over, and I naturally feel lightened and relieved. That is reality. There is no need for guilt or shame.

Rage often comes with a sense of helplessness. I feel so powerless in this situation — nothing I can do will change things. Yes, I am enraged. And I will blame everyone and everything I can for what has happened. Rage is the diffused energy of unfocused anger. Something is terribly unfinished, unresolved. As focus sharpens and energy becomes directed, rage turns into anger and becomes effective.

A woman once came to begin therapy with me because of unfocused rage that was troubling her. The night before our first session she dreamed that she was lighting my cigarettes and very angry at both me and herself for doing this. Later in our session together, it came out that her father had died of emphysema as a result of cigarette smoking. Not only had he died, but he had had to move away from his daughter to a drier climate, and she had not seen him for five years at the time of his death. All her life she had felt abandoned by her father, and the last five years of his life were the unbearable climax of a long history of being left by him. Because her real anger at him for his self-destruction and her abandonment had been so unfocused and diffuse, she had transferred her rage (and fear) onto me, dreaming that I, too, would destroy myself — and abandon her. Coming to terms with the source of her anger freed her to face new relationships with courage and faith.

Sadness is the final conflict between self-pity and compassion for oneself and others. It is not depression, for depression is a general state with no specific focus, and sadness is very focused: I am sad because of my loss, because I miss someone I loved, because I have experienced a personal diminishment. This type of highly focused sadness is the beginning of genuine self-acceptance. While self-pity wallows in sorrow, true compassion for oneself acknowledges the painful reality, the legitimacy of feeling responses, and the need for reaching out to others, and does not turn endlessly and futilely inward. My sadness can be my way out of myself, back to the human community. It can release the deadlock I have on myself which is keeping me from accepting the love and compassion of others. But first, if I'm like most people, I must experience that deadlock. We all seem to go through it this way. It is the human way toward letting go and letting be.

Primary and Secondary Feelings

These primary feelings of fear, guilt, anger, and sadness are part of the necessary process of coming to terms with grievous loss. We need to go through them to get beyond them.

Human beings have a great capacity for complicating things, and we do this most effectively by creating secondary feelings: feelings *about* feelings. In other words, we can work ourselves into feeling fearful, guilty, angry, and sad *about* our fear, guilt, anger, or sadness. Primary feelings may be necessary, but secondary feelings only get in the way. They will get you off the main track and delay the real issues. Say *no* immediately to any small voice inside you urging you toward wasting yourself in these pitfalls. Talk about your grieving process with a friend or a professional you trust, to sort out your real feelings from secondary feelings and help you keep your perspective.

What It Does

Physical Symptoms

One of the dictionary definitions of *grievous* is "causing physical suffering." Many people overlook or are surprised by the physical side of grief. It is very real and bears attending to.

The most common physical symptom of deep grief is low energy. You may need a lot of extra sleep. Be sure to allow for this. Sleep is more than "escape." Your body needs more rest, just as your soul does. You may tire more quickly than usual and feel generally fatigued. Your body may not be as dependable as usual.

You may be among the few who experience a

hyperkinetic reaction in intense bursts of physical energy. A dear friend of mine was once driven by grief to do the work of three people, to burn off her pain through physical exertion. She told me how she scrubbed her kitchen floor in the middle of the night, tears streaming into the wash bucket, working her muscles into exhaustion before she could finally find rest in a deep sleep.

You may be prey to illness. A study at Mount Sinai School of Medicine in New York in 1980 showed that the stress of bereavement can suppress the body's immune system from within two weeks following a major loss and can make a person vulnerable to illness. The work of Carl Simonton and Stephanie Matthews-Simonton also indicates particular danger periods for becoming seriously ill from eighteen months to three years following a major loss, such as the death of a spouse or an undesired retirement.

It is possible to take precautions, like the use of appropriate vitamins, proper diet, exercise, and rest; but perhaps the best precaution against the body's suffering of loss is to allow the soul the fullness of the experience. As the Simontons write in their excellent book, *Getting Well Again* (see Helpful Resources, "Grief and Disease," page 198), we can help ourselves to wholeness, or to the absorption of loss, not only by feeling the loss but by giving ourselves constant, positive messages, encouraging our organisms' self-healing functions within the limbic and the immune systems. More about this follows in the section "Expressing Grief and Taking Care of Yourself: Some Practical Suggestions."

You may notice feeling off balance, listing to one side

as you walk, being uncoordinated, having weaker vision, "mis-hearing," or "mis-seeing," especially when reading. You may experience a temporary loss of hair. Your appetite and sleeping patterns may be erratic. You may be susceptible to alcohol or other drug addiction or to overeating. You may feel "drugged" without having taken any drugs — a feeling of not being "in sync" with your own body, a looseness or coming-apart from the inside, as if your body were a bell and you were the clanger moving back and forth and around and sometimes even touching yourself from the inside of your skin.

Concentration on intense internal processes may make it difficult to navigate in the physical world. Your perception of time and distance may be slightly distorted. If this is true, you must take extra precautions in driving and using potentially dangerous tools — including fork and knife. Should any of these symptoms occur, do not be alarmed. Take care of your body. It will heal with the rest of you. See a physician for any physical symptom that worries you.

Emotional Symptoms

While you are grieving, your emotional life may be unpredictable and unstable. You may feel that there are gaps in your remembered experience; you may totally forget something you said or did and be incredulous when it is reported back to you. Your creativity may be impaired or heightened; your imagination and sense perception dulled or intensified. You may be irritable, even if this is out of character for you. You may alternate between depression and euphoria, between wailing rage and passive resignation. You may be calm and steady, but this would be surprising, if not disturbing, unless your temperament is extremely docile. If you have experienced loss and are hurting, it is reasonable that your responses will be *un*reasonable. If you see yourself as having any of the symptoms above, or if you have created your own unique emotional disruption, don't worry. The symptoms won't last forever. You will heal.

Intellectual Symptoms

You may experience impaired memory, impaired concentration, or impaired articulation. It may be more difficult than usual to communicate with others, or to say exactly what you mean — or even to know what you mean. This is temporary.

Spiritual Symptoms

If you are a person of faith, your faith may be weakened or deepened — your faith in God, in yourself, in others, in life. You may be angry — outraged — at God. You may feel closer to God and be more open to religious experience than ever before. You may feel cut off from God or from your own soul altogether. You may feel a temporary paralysis of the spirit, resulting from despair. You may be in danger of yielding to despair through physical suicide. If you feel this may be true, seek help immediately. Do not hesitate to call for someone, no matter what hour of the day or night. If you have no one, neither friend nor counselor, call the Suicide Prevention number through the operator. If you can get through the crucial hours or minutes of despair, you can get well. Hang on. Remember this. Hang on.

There is a self-destruction of the spirit that is parallel to suicide. It might be called spiritual suicide. It comes when a person shuts off the inner capacity to give or receive love. It is the most deadly result of a broken heart. I know a young woman who lived this lifeless way for ten years following her mother's death, which had occurred when the girl was fifteen. She blamed God for her mother's illness and death, and directed all her energy to hating God and loving no one.

One day when she was twenty-five years old she opened her mother's hope chest and found a letter written by her mother to her, the daughter, as a very young child. As she read the letter years later, she opened herself to the message that her mother had sent her so long ago: "I love you." In allowing herself to really hear this message, she let go of the hatred and bitterness of her loss. Her broken heart was at last allowed to mend. Once again she could love and be loved. Her buried spirit was restored to life.

Behavioral Symptoms

While you are grieving, your usual patterns of daily behavior may change or reverse, or they may become more fixed so that you can rely on routine more than before. What used to help you might not help now, and what never helped before may now be useful to you. Former habits may be disrupted or adhered to compulsively. Obsessions (addictive ways of thinking) or compulsions (addictive ways of doing) may dominate your behavior and distract you from the real pain and the real issue of your loss. Unrelated fears or fantasies may be ways of avoiding your primary pain. You may not function efficiently — or at all. You may "go on automatic" for awhile, relying on past experience and skill to accomplish your work while your heart isn't in it.

Learn to be sensitive to the changes you may be going through and be flexible with your new needs and patterns. Allow yourself to experiment with new styles of living and working that may be more appropriate for you right now. These changes need not be permanent, but if they are helpful now, use them.

Change in Attitude

You may feel "I'm not myself," and indeed you are not the self you were before the injury of loss occurred. You may have a sense of having been wounded or violated. You may feel cut off from others. In intense grief, you may feel cut off from yourself. Do not be alarmed if your attitude toward yourself and others is altered. Eventually it may be altered for the better.

The Danger of Implosion

I have already mentioned that showing emotional pain is often viewed negatively in our culture. Physical ills are more socially acceptable than emotional ills. Unfortunately many otherwise loving families have little tolerance for prolonged emotional suffering among their members. An American family will make the best of someone subjected to a month's convalescence following surgery or an acute illness, but will expect no more than a generous week for psychological recovery following an equally serious emotional injury.

There is an unspoken expectation that, while physical illness can't be helped, you are responsible for your emotional health and can control it at will. This is simply not true — or it is true only to the same extent that it is true of physical health. In order to accommodate this belief, many of us will allow our emotional pain to be transferred to the body. A psychosomatic illness is a real physical illness that has originated in the psyche and been transferred to the body because it could not otherwise be expressed.

Not only is physical pain more acceptable than emotional pain in most families, it gets more positive attention. If I say, "I feel sad today," I may get an impatient, "Shape up!" message from the person who has to live with me every day, especially if I was also sad yesterday and the day before. Understandably, my sadness can get tiresome. The strange thing is that I can have a stomach ache for three consecutive days and get fairly reliable sympathy for it. I wonder how much this social prejudice is responsible for the frequency of psychosomatic diseases in our country. The fact is simple: if I make my sadness into a physical ache, I'll be loved, and if I don't, I may be rejected. And who

47

can bear rejection on top of an already painful emotional wound?

Needless to say, sending emotional pain back down when it wants to come up and out is hard on the body and can be dangerous. When anger or fear or sadness cannot be expressed directly, it works back into the body to be expressed indirectly through some form of physical pain. This process is called retroflection: doing to myself inwardly what I want to be doing to someone or something else outwardly. I may want to strike out, to shake someone, to reach out my arms to someone, to squeeze something. And if I don't allow myself to act on this desire, I end by striking, shaking, reaching, or squeezing myself, giving myself ulcers or muscle spasms or headaches or a rash or a nervous tic.

Retroflection can be extremely self-destructive. When I come to the point where I think I cannot or dare not express feelings, when I drive emotional or spiritual feelings back down into the body, I may feel impotent, despairing, and scornful: impotent in that I believe "I can't do anything;" despairing in that I believe "If I could do something, it wouldn't do any good;" and scornful in that I feel bitter about all of this.

Such an emotional climate may turn healthy grieving into destructive disease. If the soul is not allowed to express grief, the body will do it, and the body may be harmed in the process. Medical research has linked emotional distress with cancer, arthritis, heart and thyroid disease, and colitis. One study showed that heart and stroke patients were likely to be emotionally explosive types, while cancer patients were often implosive, tending to hold themselves in and repress emotions. This same study showed that many cancer patients contracted the disease eighteen months or so following a major loss in their lives, such as the death of a spouse or retirement. Neither explosion nor implosion are good for the body, but a balanced release of emotional energy combined with good physical habits of rest, diet, and exercise combine for overall health and well-being.

The body in its wisdom creates accurate metaphors for the soul. An affliction of the heart may be physical as well as spiritual. This is by no means always the case, but when emotional injury has occurred, it is especially important to watch and listen to the warning symptoms in the body. Always it is the whole person who must be healed, for what hurts one part hurts the whole in some way.

What You Can Do about It

After recognizing how grieving feels and identifying what it does, it's time to look at what you can do about it. How can grieving be a truly healing activity and not merely a destructive passion?

Grieving is more than pain. Pain is always a symptom of some injury, an illness or a woundedness. Pain in grief is a symptom of the spiritual wound caused by loss. To tend to the wound is to heal oneself through the creative struggle and final assimilation of the reality of the loss by the whole physical and spiritual person.

Paradoxically, the way past the pain is to go all the way through it. To treat the symptom of pain by the distractions of frantic busy-ness, compulsive overdrinking or overeating, or other dulling, self-destructive behavior is only a way of prolonging the healing process. We really hurt more when we try compulsively to hurt less. Still, there are ways to work through pain by grieving well, rather than through the tail-spinning, destructive hurting of avoidance and denial. This constructive kind of hurting is what we feel when we lance an infected wound or pour iodine over a cut. And there are ways to bring about healing which are not necessarily painful.

Expressing Grief and Taking Care of Yourself:
Some Practical Suggestions

At the very beginning of a grief process, become aware of ways in which you unnecessarily and self-destructively hurt yourself. For instance, when you hold yourself in, choke back tears, tighten facial and throat muscles, swallow down surging emotions, or suffocate feelings — *it hurts*. And it doesn't "hurt good." *It hurts bad.* It hurts in the way a physical wound would hurt if instead of responding to the pain and bleeding you ignored it and allowed dirt and gravel to get into it — and then, even worse, if you actually ground the dirt and gravel down deep into the wound. You need to treat a spiritual wound resulting from loss as carefully and realistically as you would treat any physical wound. The treatment would of course vary, as with a physical wound, depending on its depth and degree.

Nature gives us two warning signs when we have

been injured, one knowable only to us, and one that is also visible to others. The first sign is pain, and the second is bleeding. We also have pain and the equivalent of bleeding in our emotional or spiritual beings. Sometimes injury involves no pain, but serious bleeding, as in a clean and serious severance caused by some forms of amputation. The same is true on an emotional or spiritual level. The important thing is to pay attention to the signs, and to act wisely and immediately to respond to the reality of the injury.

The worst thing that can happen with any wound is to ignore it so that it becomes infected. Then one is not only in danger from the original wound, but also from one's own defense mechanisms. The body's response to infection is to produce increasing amounts of white blood cells to work as defensive warriors, antibodies clustering around the offending invasion of germ organisms. As the body is multiplying its own defenses, tremendous amounts of extra energy may be required, depending on the extent of the wound and the intensity of the infection. A fever may result. An untended fever can cause serious damage to the organism — even death. Again, the same is true emotionally. Treating an emotional wound involves avoiding the neglect that may result in being hurt, even endangered, by your own defenses.

Ultimately, the injured organism heals itself. Your body has its own healing wisdom within it. So does your soul — the expressive container of your emotional life. Two vital external things are essential to the self-healing process: time and cooperation.

Time speaks for itself. A line from a popular song

says so truly, "What a friend we have in time."* The friendship of time will be described in more detail later on.

Cooperation is what *you* bring to the healing process. First you locate the injury. Then you find out what makes the injury worse (like walking too soon with a broken ankle). Then, very simply, *don't do* whatever hurts and makes the wound worse. Instead, brace yourself to do the painful but necessary things to treat the injury.

Likewise, find out what makes you feel better, and learn the difference between a feeling better that is really healing (smoothing ointment onto a burn or spooning nourishing soup into your sick body), and a feeling better that is fake, counterproductive and self-destructive (scratching a poison ivy rash). Again, very simply, do what feels better and is also healing; don't do what only feels better for a moment and is damaging in the long run.

The essential treatment after sustaining the injury of a loss is that you express fully what the loss means to you. Not expressing grief can lead to depression, repression, and even unconscious oppression of yourself and others. Seek out persons you trust — close friends or relatives or competent professional persons. Talk to them about your loss and its meaning. Talk until you have exhausted talk. Before you wear out the patience of your friends, relatives, or professional helpers, or

*From the song "Friends With You" by Bill Danoff and Taffy Nivert, sung by John Denver on the RCA stereo record *Aerie*.

become boring even to yourself, there is much that can be said — and the saying of it will help heal the wound. What you cannot say, write. Keep a journal. I once began a journal after many years away from the practice. It was a grief journal. I used it solely for the self-therapy of grieving. The blank paper could reject none of my pain and was never bored by it the way another human being might have been.

Besides talking, let yourself cry — as often as needed. You need not cry in front of others if this inhibits you. First let yourself cry in private. Then, gradually, entrust your tears to another person. Let yourself ask to be held. Let yourself be held. But choose the person you ask wisely. Someone who can be a mother or a father figure is usually an ideal choice. This is especially important for men. If you are a man reading this, consider yourself herewith permitted to cry, often, alone and with others, and in someone else's arms. If you are a man, it may be wonderfully healing to let yourself cry in the arms of another man. It's always better to cry in someone else's presence than to do so alone. In deep pain or genuine sorrow this is true not because you need an audience, but because you need a witness to your pain — a witness in the religious sense. You need someone to testify to the validity of your feelings, to acknowledge them, and to say yes to the good work you are doing in expressing them.

If you feel too ashamed to cry much in front of other persons, or if you worry that you will bore them with your tears, place yourself in the presence of God, however you may conceive of God, and entrust your tears to that presence. There is a beautiful saying: "As

God is my witness." If this is not possible for you, imagine a loving human presence, the memory of someone whose love you have experienced, and let that presence stand by you as you weep. Sometimes, even a pet can be a sustaining comfort when one is distressed and weeping.

If you are a person who doesn't cry — or if you know you need to cry but can't for some reason in this particular situation — an outside stimulus for catharsis may be useful. A movie, play, piece of music, or book may trigger tears unexpectedly. If you begin crying for a character in a movie or piece of literature, or weeping over a situation in a song — no matter how inane it may seem to you — let it be. Let yourself yield to the expressive emotion, recognizing that you have begun to weep for yourself, and thus have reached an important stage in self-healing. Weeping is only a stage; it won't last forever. You needn't be afraid to cry.

Crying is what you do when you can't do anything else — before you are able to find other ways to express your grief. It is better than doing nothing, for then your body will internalize the tears and you may become ill, experiencing actual bodily symptoms. The body creates vivid metaphors. It may substitute other forms of "weeping" — releasing inner excesses in liquid form. Catching a cold, developing watering eyes and draining sinuses are obvious symbols of a release that needs to happen emotionally. My Russian mother told me that the Russians have a saying: "Tears are the baptism of the soul." To be baptized means to be cleansed, to be reborn.

If your loss cuts deep, or if it is an old loss that has

been buried alive without ever having been fully grieved over, it is important that you not be alone when you do specific grief work. Have human resources available for comfort and reassurance. If you descend far down into your deep or old pain, you will need someone physically present to help bring you back up, to reconnect with reality in the present. A skilled therapist or an understanding friend will be an absolutely necessary companion on a journey deep into an intensely felt loss. Facing your loss can be a death-like experience. You must provide sources of new life for yourself when you come out the other side. You will be as fresh, and perhaps as fragile, as a newborn infant.

Talking and crying are fundamental means of self-expression. They allow feelings contained in the body as energy to be released as genuine emotion — energy that literally *moves out*, presses upward and is uttered or "outered" through the body's natural functions of speech and tears.

Though it may strike you as unnecessary, I want to remind you of the most essential bodily function in connection with grieving — breathing. It is the source of all life. Yet when we are weighed heavily with the burden of strong and painful feelings, breathing is what we first forget to do. I have seen clients doing grief work in therapy who will unconsciously hold their breath for a minute or more, or who slow down their breathing to the point of losing color, but are still unaware of what they are doing to themselves — literally cutting off their own life source. I find it necessary to interrupt them in their work with regular reminders: keep breathing, keep breathing. This becomes common punctuation in the therapeutic encounter.

Depriving the brain and other vital organs of necessary oxygen is not only physically damaging, but also interferes with important mental and psychological processes. This deprivation is another way in which people hurt themselves. Instead of swallowing pain, or containing it in tensed muscles, it is literally buried, suffocated in the psychic coffin of the life-deprived body. If you are grieving, make "keep breathing" your mantra. If you don't know how to breathe fully from the diaphragm, find someone who can teach you and practice it with dedication and discipline until it is natural to you. Then your body will make you conscious of what you are doing when you fail to breathe fully and rhythmically. Keep breathing!

To breathe from the diaphragm, lie on your back and put your hand on your diaphragm, just above your navel and over your lower ribs. When you inhale, you should feel and see your hand rise. Most people breathe this way naturally while lying down. Now sit up and do the same thing. Do your shoulders rise when you inhale? If so, your breathing is shallow. Take the air in more deeply until you feel and see your hand being pushed outward, and your shoulders are steady as you breathe.

A good way to release tension is to breathe it out. Where is the tension in your body? Where are you tight and withholding? Imagine that you are breathing in and out of that part of your body — perhaps your neck, hands, or buttocks. Feel the tightness of the muscles there, and imagine that as you breathe, the air opens and soothes the tightness, removing the debris of tension with each exhalation. Literally blow the tension out of that part of your body as you let it breathe.

Concentration on one's breathing is the simplest way to let go of tensions. It hurts to hold oneself tight, to press back painful feelings instead of expressing them, but it's not always easy to stop doing this. Desperation can result if one simply doesn't know how to let go, or if one wants to but is afraid that the dam will burst — that if a little is released, all of what is inside will flood forth and overwhelm the person. It's usually true that feelings which are finally expressed are not nearly so frightening or overwhelming as feelings which are not faced, and which remain in the world of the unknown where hidden things always seem more powerful than they really are.

It is possible, even with the pressure of strong feelings just below the surface, to allow oneself to untighten, to unclench, to release and relax without being over-whelmed or destroyed by uncontrollable emotions. The way to protect yourself is first to acknowledge that the emotions exist. Thus recognized, they will not be so inclined to haunt or taunt you as when they are denied and must create a disturbance to get attention and respect. Often the clamor we sense just below the surface subsides in great measure once we own our painful feelings. This makes it possible to begin dealing with those feelings, bit by bit. Have faith in yourself. Your body has a wisdom that will call your attention to important aspects of your life that you may be ignoring, and your soul has the same wisdom. Paying attention to this wisdom is the beginning of healing.

The wisdom of the body expresses itself through physical means, and the wisdom of the soul expresses itself through fantasies and dreams. Dreams represent the wisdom of the soul or psyche in working through the total reality of a person's life — past, present, and future. They are marvelously structured creations, spontaneous works of art, and taken as a whole they often reveal striking patterns of ingenuity and originality in their gift of unfolding revelation.

The great analyst, Carl Jung, followed Freud in a deep appreciation of the healing value of dreams. He taught himself to listen and to see — to attend to the vocabulary of the soul as it is revealed in dream metaphors, symbols, and images. Dreams are a form of self-expression from our inner selves, and they can also be the means through which God touches us, to give us comfort and guidance.

The function of dreams is as manifold as that of any other form of communication. They may help us to resolve conflict, to experience the pleasure of fulfilled wishes, to show us what we fear — the functions most frequently dealt with in the work of Freud. And they may bring us into the richness of the communion of saints — the great invisible network of human thought and feeling, aspiration and growth, in harmony with the intent of our Creator (see page 113). This is the level of dream function with which Jung worked.

Dreams may also be mundane and random patterns of reworking and resolving images from daily life, with varying degrees of meaning. Not all dreams are of equal significance, and it is important to bring our conscious powers of discernment to the meeting with our dream-selves. I view dialogue with one's dreams as dream appreciation, not presuming to interpret a gift from the soul anymore than I would "interpret" a friend. Rather I listen, play with the patterns, and learn from the metaphors which emerge from my or my client's deeper self, in order to understand life, and to become an ever more lively participant in the human adventure.

Earlier I mentioned the helpfulness of keeping a journal — writing down all your secret feelings and impressions, your doubts and fears, your hopes and longings, the private exploration of meaning as you live your life from day to day. Writing these things down gives credence to your life's process of becoming whole, and the act of writing becomes especially validating in times of crisis or injury. In this activity of grieving, you become your own physician. The journal is a record of your spiritual self-therapy — as a physician's record might record your participation in and response to physical therapy. It shows that you are indeed on a journey — a journey toward healing and renewal. The journal can be the map of your journey, charted from your own unique discovery of the way.

I find the similarity between the words *journal* and *journey* a significant one. The spiritual journal is a record of the spiritual journey. The most common guideposts on this journey come to us from our own unconscious in the form of dreams. Dreams tell us the truth about ourselves as we can bear to hear it, and they show us signs of being lost or being true as we travel toward healing and wholeness. They tell us what we need to know through images that are more or less clear according to our receptivity. We can become more receptive to our own truth as we enter into relationship with the gift of the dream. One way to do this is to write the dream down, in the present tense, as an important part of a journal.

I write my dreams in my journal, and then I copy (type) them after a few days of "walking around in them" or reliving them from different perspectives, and I bring the fuller understanding of my conscious experience of the unconscious gift into a special dream journal. In this way, I have an ongoing record of dreams which enables me readily to see the patterns of my dreams — recurring images, feelings, figures, animals, people, colors, words, and motifs. I find that there is a continuing "cast of characters" in the ongoing drama of my dreams. As I enter into relationship with them, I create new wholeness between my conscious and unconscious energies by bringing these vital parts of myself into a give and take relationship, a stimulating dialogue. This is never more healing or productive as in times of emotional injury, as in grievous loss.

It is also helpful to tell a dream to a trusted friend, a spiritual confidant, or a professional therapist or pastor. A person who can function in my life as a dream-mate is valuable and precious not because she or he can interpret dreams for me (only parts of the dreamer's self can do that), but because having a dream-mate lets me claim the reality of my own soul by telling my dream as an actual story and reliving it out loud before a witness. This is why I suggested earlier that when writing down the dream it is best to use the present tense. A dream is not something you "had." It is something you create, and something that re-creates you, and does so with greater clarity and effectiveness as you consciously relive it and associate it with all your meanings in an awake state. As you share your dream with a dream-mate, re-experience it in the present tense. Astounding new insights, meanings, and connections can be made from this simple act.

Telling or writing the dream several times allows for the emergence of more meaning. A dream is like a poem, a tremendously concentrated and economical structure compacting content that could otherwise fill books. Its richness is in its economy and its precision in choosing particular images. This makes returning to it again and again a profitable experience.

Grieving dreams are especially full, though they may become tedious to the dreamer, for the work they do is not easily accomplished. The destination of the dream-journey is healing, and this may require going through an open wound again and again, to cleanse it thoroughly, and finally to mend it. Sometimes this can feel as if you are performing surgery on yourself without an anesthetic. Other times it seems mercifully less painful. The point is that you are ultimately the only one who can do this healing work for yourself, whether it is surgery of the soul or merely rehabilitative spiritual therapy. You as dreamer are the physician within your own soul, doing a sacred work while the body rests.

When you have been injured, your own deepest self will rally to your support. Your soul will find ways of taking care of you, helping you to heal from the inside out. The deeper the injury, the deeper the healing. Dreams will take good care of you if you cooperate with them. You are the producer of your dreams. Pay attention to what you have produced, to the truth you tell yourself. Your dreams will never tell you more than you can bear.

You can hear and see even more from dreams by completing them in a waking state, getting back into the dream and allowing images, conversations, and actions to come up that were not in the original dream. The "revised" or "revisited" dream can lead you into more and more awareness about your own needs, blocks, and sources of support.

You have external sources of support also. Begin to recognize these, and to reach out actively to them and use them. Let yourself be cared for by others. Rely on friendships to carry you through hard times. Learn to express deeper levels of trust with your loved ones. It will be an honor for them to help you. Don't deprive them of this honor. Let yourself ask for help of all sorts — practical and spiritual — from your friends, family, co-workers, and skilled professionals. They are there for you, with gifts of time, wisdom, support, and love. They will understand if you can be honest about your pain because they too have had pain in life. Often they will be eager to help you in ways that others have helped them. Don't miss opportunities for developing and deepening relationships in critical moments of your life.

Since your energy level may be quite low, your resources generally pulled inward for self-healing, don't push yourself physically or emotionally. Stay with your normal routine but limit yourself just as you would if you were convalescing from a physical injury. Maintain your life but don't take on anything extra. You need all your energy to do the essential healing work. It's perfectly all right to "go on automatic" for awhile. Count on your own skills and past experiences to get you through your usual work. Once when I had suffered a horrible loss through the end of a relationship, I had to get through two difficult days of lecturing, poetry readings, and press conferences. I had no energy at all and was sure that I'd never be able to do my work, or to do it well at any rate. Between lectures and conferences I excused myself for a few minutes and went off to cry alone. I returned and miraculously I came through for myself and for the people for whom I had promised to do this work. I was able to rely on the years of previous experience. Even though what I was doing was routine for me, it was new for the people I was with at the time.

During the times when "automatic" doesn't work for you, let others know what you are going through and ask for help, or ask someone else to take over for you until you can gather your energy again for the task. I told the people who had asked me to speak that I was having a hard time because of a recent traumatic loss. They were touched that I had confided in them and given them an opportunity to respond to me and minister to my needs. This made for mutuality in our relationship. They could do something for me as well as receive something from me. The experience was actually enhanced by my sharing the reality of my pain with them.

While you are grieving, you are in the process of restoring your basic capacity for life. You won't experience great joys or intense pleasures, but for the time being you can learn to substitute simply satisfying comforts for these. Develop a new appreciation for the simple sustaining gifts of life — for walking, breathing, sleeping; for nourishing food and kind friends. Mere physical well-being can take on new meaning and value for you. Relying on the constancy of your own human life processes can be a working substitute for the joys of life from which you are temporarily cut off.

Focus your conscious energy on cooperating with your body's efforts to help and heal you. Avoid emotional strains of all sorts and concentrate on very basic life-sustaining things. Discipline yourself to eat nourishing meals regularly, to get the full amount of sleep that you need (you may need extra sleep for awhile) and to exercise in your usual manner. If you don't usually exercise, make it a point now to go for short walks each day out of doors in fresh air. Don't take on anything strenuous. Keep it simple. If you enjoy swimming, find a way occasionally to swim in a heated pool. Nothing is more healing that water, and swimming relaxes the muscles like no other activity.

You may want to take extra vitamins while you are going through the stressful experience. Sometimes when you feel particularly shaky or weak, the cause may be physical more than emotional, and simply eating an orange, a piece of cheese, or a mixture of raisins and nuts can restore you quickly by replenishing necessary potassium, calcium, or protein to your body. Try warm milk, Postum, or herbal teas at bedtime to help soothe you to sleep.

Avoid physical excesses as you avoid emotional strains. Don't put too much or too little of any good thing into your body, and don't overdo on healthy activities.

Since it will be hard to remember all these good things to do for your body, you might want to organize a moderate regimen of healthy activities for youself on a checklist. Help yourself return to the basics by scheduling three meals a day and giving yourself extra vitamins with one of your meals. It may be helpful to tape a small checklist over your kitchen sink or in some other convenient spot to remind you to take care of yourself each day. Remember, while grieving you are dealing with a loss that you can't do anything about, but you *can* do something about yourself.

You can heal your attitude with affirmations, as I suggested earlier. My favorite way to do this involves working with two affirmations at a time for one week. At the end of the week, they may be continued, or one or both of them changed if the affirmation seems to have become part of oneself. Determine the affirmation that you most need. It may be something like: "I am a beautiful child of God," or "I am a beloved child of God," or "I deserve to receive love and respect," or "I can act effectively in my own behalf," or "I do not have to punish myself," or "I deserve to be happy," or "I have the power to change my life for the good." Write the affirmation and tape it on your mirror. If you can, for ten minutes before bedtime and upon rising in the morning, look at your image in the mirror and say the affirmation out loud. You make it real by uttering it forth into the world, and you are your own witness as you see and hear yourself say it.

During this affirmation, there may be "background

noise" from your subconscious, as if someone were playing a radio in the background. This may take the form of ridicule, shame, embarrassment, or denial. You may recognize faces or voices of specific people in your present or past, or your own face or voice at a certain age or in a certain mood. Do not argue with the background noise. Let it be and simply proceed with the affirmation. At the end of the session, make a note to yourself as to the origin and nature of the background noise. From day to day, observe any changes in it. A ridiculing teacher or a nasty peer who caused a fuss on the first day of your affirmations may be silenced by the fourth, gone by the sixth, and back cheering you on by the eighth. Should the background noise be too loud or distracting, create a band of allies, people whom you know believe in you and would support your affirmation, and let *them* defend you against the rowdies, so that you can carry on, persevering in your affirmation. A week may do it, or you may want to continue for several months, until the message is truly a part of you.

Choose a second affirmation and work on it at the same time in this way: Each day, go to a favorite safe and pleasant place with a glass of water or something else pleasant to sip. Use good paper and different colored pens that please you, and write this affirmation seventy times a day for seven days. Then it is yours. You have worked it into your muscles and nerves: from brain to hand to eye to brain. Pause frequently to sip your drink and enjoy your surroundings. You are teaching yourself a new message, a positive attitude, and the method of your teaching is not punishment, but play.

To heal a specific hurt: If it is part of your body, lovingly touch it with your hand, close your eyes and visualize it healed, and bathe that image in white light, then in pink for soothing, and say, "Bless you, be healed." If it is an emotional hurt, construct a *manageable image* for it, close your eyes and bathe the image in the white and then pink light and say, "Bless you, be healed." Observe how the image responds and changes as you continue from day to day.

Create an image — either from memory or through fantasy — of a favorite, happy and safe place, and take yourself there for mini-retreats or vacations throughout the day, even if only for a few seconds. Enjoy that place within you. Fill it in as fully as you can, using all of your senses. How does it look, sound, smell? Be at peace, be comforted. This is your place, and you have it always within you. Here you are always welcomed and at home.

Here are some suggestions for other specific things you can do which may be helpful:

If someone has died, write down all the good things you can remember about the person; write down all the loving things the person said or did to you or for you, past or recent, as he or she stands out in your memory. Resist the temptation to indulge in guilt or doubt. Instead, memorialize the graces of the person and of your relationship.

Take care of someone or something outside yourself, even early on, but keep it simple: care for a plant, or a pet, or do something nice for a friend or neighbor, even

if it's only making a pot of coffee. Something in the universe needs you and depends on you. You are a useful human being!

Work outside. Keep a garden or take on a sport, but keep it simple.

Do handcrafts if you already know them and find them relaxing. Make something for someone who's been especially kind to you.

Early on, large muscle work can help, such as painting walls or fences — work that is even and rhythmic, but not too strenuous.

Visit the zoo. Spend time observing the large animals. (If your local zoo isn't a very good one, don't go. Seeing animals in cages can be depressing. But watching them going about in a natural space can remind us of what it is to be a good, basic human animal.)

Spend time watching fish in an aquarium. Start an aquarium if you're so inclined. It's better than television!

Hug trees. They are very healing beings. It's also healing to sit or stand with your back leaning against a tree for awhile, to restore peace to your being. A tree will let you squeeze it without being hurt, giving you a loving outlet for aggression. A client of mine once dreamed that she hugged a tree and it began to give forth honey, feeding and nourishing her from its very veins. *Let nature nurture you.*

Groan in the shower. Imagine a waterfall, washing away the pain and fatigue, covering you and filling you with peace, power, protection.

Have a professional massage — the restorative equivalent of eight hours of good sleep!

See your physician for help with any physical problems.

See a psychotherapist for support if you have no one as an immediate witness to your pain and process, or if you feel suicidal or that you can't cope alone.

See your pastor or another person who functions as a spiritual resource in your life.

Avoid all forms of self-torture, self-punishment, and self-neglect.

Avoid external stimuli that make you feel worse.

Listen to music but not Rachmaninoff. Baroque and classical music have a most soothing effect, due to their orderly patterns. Mozart and Haydn are very healing. If a love relationship has broken, avoid popular ballads and the score of *Camelot!* (Don't worry. You'll be able to enjoy Rachmaninoff, Chopin, Sibelius, and show music again. Just not now.)

Avoid heaviness. Choose only light (but not giddy) books, movies, plays and television programs.

Beware of smoking, drinking, eating too much, or using drugs. (This is a time when you may be especially susceptible to becoming dependent upon pain-dulling drugs, even those which may have been prescribed by a physician.)

Give yourself small kindnesses and comforts, such as oil baths, special teas, or favorite comfort foods. Buy yourself something new. If you spend extra money on yourself right now, you're worth it. (Don't be foolish in spending though. If you can't afford a new car or a new silk outfit, don't buy one, or you'll hurt yourself more in the long run. Be generous, but realistic.)

Your body and soul are analogous. Give your soul

vitamins too. Your body needs high potency vitamins when it undergoes stress, and your soul needs emotional megavitamins — large doses of things which nourish your feeling life, emotional vitamins for the eyes, ears, touch, taste and smell. Give yourself the sight of healing mountains and animals, the sound and sight of water, fine music, good food, and favorite-feeling clothes to wear. This is not indulgence; it's therapy, and you are your own best therapist because you know best what helps you.

If you feel stuck, do something new.

If you feel empty, gradually fill the space in yourself with interests, people, projects. Not too much too soon, but make a steady commitment to yourself to take action.

Value the grieving work you are doing. It's important!

Finally and most importantly, discover what helps you. No one else can do this for you.

Pace yourself lovingly. *Remember, this pain won't last forever.*

Be sensitive to your own timing. Don't push yourself ahead of your process, and don't let others push you because they are uncomfortable with your grief. Let it take as long as it takes. Don't hold on either. Let the pain go when the time comes. Doing grief work is like being a trapeze artist: balance and timing are everything. Letting go too soon and holding on too long are equally dangerous.

Learn to tolerate the tedium and clumsiness of the process.

Trust time. Time is on your side.

Enjoy good memories. Poems and people are powerful in the remembering. Memories ground us in our humanity. Let go of the pain of the past and tell stories to help you reclaim the good. Fantasy can be useful. Allow yourself to talk out loud to whomever or whatever you have lost, describing what that person or thing meant to you and means to you now through the experience of loss.

Gradually, reclaim your power to create, to imagine, to perceive, to define, to believe.

Regain yourself, your freedom to live again.

After Dismembering

Not fixed perfection but
again-and-again completion,
unfolding, open-circling.

To re-member your Self
is to for-get
to get(Be)fore pain
to what you are
deeper down.

To re-member your Self
is to for-give,
to give(Be)fore to yourself
blessing: healing from
the wound by means of the wound
itself; and
comfort: deep strength with
deep peace.

Bless you, Be comforted.
From the moment
that holds you,
begin anew.

Four

Four Styles of Grieving

You and I are unique individuals. We respond differently to the same set of circumstances. Different people
and different things hold different meanings for each of
us. And yet we are similar in many ways. We share a
common human nature. We are physical, spiritual,
emotional, and intellectual in our make-up. We are
both strong (in different ways) and vulnerable (in
different ways). We share an ability to communicate,
though our communicating styles may be quite different.

If both of us were faced with an identical loss — the
loss of a job, for instance — our responses might be
surprisingly different, or strangely similar. Your initial
response might be an optimistic assurance that you can
go out and get any new job you want. My response
might be to imagine myself destitute twenty years from
now! Or we both might be crushed for a day or two,
and then begin to explore new possibilities with confi-

dence and determination. How we do respond to the situation of a grievous loss will depend largely on our own basic temperament and the effect that the sum of our separate experiences has had on each of us.

In my observation of the grieving process, four distinct styles of grieving have become recognizable to me. Despite our differences — the constitutional uniqueness of each of us — our common human nature will probably incline us toward one general grieving attitude or style should we find ourselves confronted with painful loss. We may take the attitude of the Hero, the Martyr, the Crazyperson, or the Fool. We may shift from one style to another, going through all four styles as we complete our process, or alternating between a combination of any two of them. Or we may remain consistently with one grieving style, changing and growing according to the mode of that particular figure.

Each of the four styles has a negative and a positive phase. It may be helpful to consider both aspects of each figure or style in order to understand them more clearly.

It may also be helpful to remember the four feeling stages — fear, guilt, rage, and sadness — common to those who grieve. These stages come *in between* the shock of loss and the renewed well-being which follows the healing process of realization. First, in severe loss which is the same as severe injury, there is shock — numbness, non-feeling; then feelings emerge, first in confusion, and gradually as distinct, clear emotional states that may succeed one another in any order, or may overlap and occasionally be felt simultaneously again. Through allowing oneself to experience these feelings and to integrate them fully with the rest of one's being, pain is gradually released and the ability to live life is regained. Well-being is restored.

For most people, then, the grieving process progresses like this:

> shock
>
> four feeling stages: fear, guilt, rage, sadness
>
> well-being

It is in the feeling stages of this process that the four styles of grieving become apparent. The relationship of these grieving styles to the four corresponding feeling stages will become clear as we examine each style in its negative and positive aspects. Each style offers a way of individual development through the experience of loss, and no style is "better" than any other. The styles are simply different, each one better suited to a particular person at a particular time — and even then, with great room for variation within each style. They are simply ways of generalizing in order to understand and have confidence in the process.

The Hero

The kind of heroic stance one assumes depends on how one faces fear, either by acknowledging it or denying that it exists. The negative side of heroics is isolation from others based on denial. The person who denies fear is a mock hero and becomes the ultimate victim of fear, for he or she feels compelled toward defiance in order to prove a fearlessness that doesn't exist. By pretending to be the victor in the face of fear, the mock hero falls victim to it because every move must then be determined by the sole motive of proving a bravery that is false. The mock hero is so afraid of feelings that he or she will deny having them. The mock hero says "I can handle this — alone." The theme is conquest through control. The results are often tragic.

Mock heroics can begin very early and are frequently learned unconsciously. A friend recently told me the devastating story of her foster son. Thirty years ago, when her foster son was five years old, he and his three-year-old brother were paying their weekly visit to their mother, who was a patient in a tuberculosis sanitorium. When they arrived the head nurse gently informed them that their mother had died during the night. The three-year-old shouted at her, "I don't believe it, I don't believe it!" He ran to his mother's room, saw her empty bed, and began to sob. The elder brother stood motionless, making no response at all, and he refused to look in her room. Throughout the following days of funeral and burial, the elder brother continued unmoved.

As the boys grew, the younger brother proved well-adjusted, but the elder brother suffered over every small change. In his teens, he was diagnosed as having psychotic tendencies. In his twenties, he committed murder in a psychotic episode, randomly shooting a farmer and all the farm animals in sight. After his release from prison ten years later, he committed a second brutal crime, raping and murdering an old woman and shooting a twelve-year-old boy. He claims to remember nothing of either incident. Psychiatric tests indicate a strong relationship between the violent outbursts and the repression of grief over his mother's death when he was a very young child.

Afraid to face reality, the false hero simply denies it and carries on as if nothing happened — until tragedy strikes. I know of a man who impressed his acquaintances with his quiet dignity following the death of his wife and child in an auto accident from which he escaped unharmed. After calmly finishing arrangements for their funeral, he killed himself. Perhaps his death could have been avoided if he had found a safe outlet for his grief.

The negative and dangerous side of the heroic posture is what I have called mock heroics, the denial of fear and the denial of feelings. This is often based on some essential distrust of one's self, a deep doubt that one could endure the loss or survive the pain if one truly faced it. Extremely sensitive persons are often susceptible to this attitude. It can be paralyzing. The intense introversion — turning inward — of fear has a freezing effect on the soul, and on the personality of the individual. It is such a dangerous position with potential for violence and destruction because it is a false position. In order to preserve itself, every genuine emotion which might betray it is driven inward, where that emotion is not destroyed but rather stored for the future. The mock hero is a walking time bomb with no clue as to the date of detonation.

There is, on the other hand, a genuinely heroic stance in response to grievous loss. This is the positive side of the heroic attitude. The real hero is someone who acknowledges fear, and then goes ahead and does what is necessary. True courage is not the absence of fear, but an honest recognition of fear combined with a deep trust, either in one's self or in someone or something outside one's self, that makes the fear bearable and appropriate action possible. The real hero is able to act appropriately because of trust, as the mock hero is unable to act appropriately because of distrust. The truly heroic attitude in grief is one which says, "I trust in myself to be able to suffer and to be supported by others, and I trust others to support me." The real hero is able to stand alone against fear realistically because he or she is able to reach out toward others: "I am the only one who can do this suffering for myself, but there are others all around me to give me strength and love. I know that I need them, and I accept both my need and their love." This attitude accepts the real nobility of self and others. It offers a way of bearing reality with grace.

The genuine hero faces fear and feelings and does what is necessary. In grief, what is necessary is to suffer one's loss with faith. To one who perseveres, understanding and acceptance will come. In facing loss that is severe, sometimes the best outcome is being able to see that there are things in life which are neither understandable nor acceptable — and in understanding and accepting that, real peace can come.

The Martyr

In the negative sense, the martyr knows all there is to know about guilt — except how to get rid of it. The introverted martyr blames himself or herself and proceeds to deal out a self-punishment program that would make the penal code of the Spanish Inquisition seem mild.

The mock martyr is implosive, turning the energy of guilt inward, retroflecting emotional pain and frequently making herself or himself sick. Causing pain to oneself is a substitute for suffering the reality of loss.

Often the guilt-ridden person will ask the question, "Why didn't it happen to *me*?" A woman in her forties joined a grief group to work on unresolved guilt that went back to her childhood. She and her younger sister were raised by strict missionary parents in Africa. Her sister contracted a serious infection, but the parents refused to take the child to the medical compound or give her any kind of treatment, since this was against their religious principles. The child eventually recovered, but remained horribly crippled from the disease for the rest of her life. Every member of the family became the devoted servant of the disabled one, trying to make her life better. The elder sister grew up with the constant image of the contrast between her robust health and her sister's misery. Her life was burdened more with pity for her sister than with the physical service she provided her from day to day.

As an adult the question, "Why her and not me?" began to haunt her. For twenty years of her adult life, this healthy older sister suffered one debilitating symptom after another and several emotional breakdowns as she reached her forties. It was as if she were trying to substitute herself for her innocent sister by suffering in her place. As a child, the older sister may have actually felt that she had no right to be healthy and whole while her sister suffered so. And in time, she came to resent her younger sister bitterly for being the cause of such emotional anguish.

Resentment is the natural child of guilt. Ultimately we resent what makes us feel guilty. It is heartbreaking that, in the name of religion, and doubtless in ignorance, a double cruelty was committed. One daughter was made to suffer needless physical crippling, and the other daughter was made to bear needless emotional crippling. In time, through years of confronting the situation in its entirety, the older daughter was able to achieve physical and emotional wholeness.

One of my clients came for her first session two years after her husband's death. During that time, she had secretly blamed and punished herself for failing to call an ambulance in time. Her husband was an alcoholic who died of a hemorrhage resulting from the disease. He didn't tell his wife that he was bleeding and refused to let her call for help. It was only when he passed out that she took matters into her own hands, and only after his death that she knew the extent of his illness. But in retrospect, she took on all the responsibility for his death, when in fact he himself was responsible. She was finally able to see this and let go of her unrealistic guilt. This allowed her to express her legitimate anger toward her husband, which in turn allowed her to feel reconciled with him and his death, and freed her to be a happier living person.

The word *martyr* comes from the Greek word meaning "witness." A martyr in the purest sense is a witness to reality. We are so accustomed to the historical equation of martyrdom with willing death or self-sacrifice (which often has the unfortunate effect of making all survivors feel guilty!) that we are totally unaware of this literal meaning of the word. In its original sense, it has nothing to do with death or self-sacrifice. It simply means someone who serves as a witness to the truth. The positive aspect of the martyr style of grieving is in this literal sense. The genuine martyr-witness sees what is and, in so seeing realistically, is able to recognize where responsibilities lie — where one's own responsibilities end and the responsibilities of others begin. The woman who came to see me was able to let go of her guilt when she saw her own and her husband's responsibilities clearly. She changed from being a martyr in the negative sense to being a real witness to the truth of her situation. In seeing and speaking that truth, she became free.

The Crazyperson

If the mock martyr is a master at self-blame, the negatively oriented crazyperson's style is to blame everyone else. Extroverted rage lashes out blindly in all directions, causing pain to others with the same efficiency of the martyr for self-inflicted pain.

The crazyperson's style is explosive and attacking. Unfocused rage rules the day. Feelings crash indiscriminately together in a baffling outward display of undirected wrath. To others, such behavior seems damaging and self-indulgent; to the enraged person, it can be disconcerting and self-destructive. The negative phase of the crazyperson's style often finds him or her lashing out at friends and loved ones who could be most supportive. Unless they are possessed with the patience of angels, they are likely to be alienated or frightened away. The crazyperson effectively cuts off his or her best support systems.

A grief-stricken woman was enraged over the circumstances of her spouse's death for nearly three years. Granted, they were enraging circumstances. The man had been suffering a nameless and mounting anxiety for several weeks when he agreed to consult a psychiatrist. At the end of the first — and only — consultation, the doctor prescribed a powerful drug, one normally administered to institutionalized psychotics. Eight hours after his first dose of the drug, the man jumped off a bridge. His wife, in her despair, lashed out at all the wrong people, alienating many of her friends and her own children by her prolonged irritability and repeated explosions.

Finally, after three years, she told a group of artist associates about her husband's tragic death. One of the women in the group, a psychiatrist, asked the name of the drug which her husband had been given. When told, she turned purple and said that the prescription was completely wrong for his symptoms, that the doctor should not be permitted to get by without censure. Hearing this, the woman began to focus her unfocused rage sharply on the person who should have been held responsible all along. In her movement from undirected rage to direct anger, she finally was able to come to terms with her grief.

A person may need to experience rage as part of the process of achieving authentic anger. In grieving, "acting crazy" may be one step toward "going sane." In this woman's case, explosion and attack were appropriate, but she was directing them inappropriately. Once she became focused, the function of her anger became effective, and the genuine outcry of her soul was heard where it needed to be heard. An initial explosive response that may seem "crazy" to others may in fact be a constructive response to an insane situation.

Rage comes from a sense of deep frustration and powerlessness; the change from rage to anger means the transformation from powerlessness to power — the ability to act effectively again.

The Fool

If the negative question of the martyr is "Why not me?" the negative question of the fool is "Why me?"

The fool's style of grieving is related to the feeling stage of sadness. The negative aspect of the fool is seen in a distorted expression of sadness in either of two ways: by covering it up with a pretense of gaiety, or by allowing oneself to be consumed by sadness to an extreme.

The fool can avoid sadness by playing the clown, hiding an isolating self-pity with a mask of jokes and joviality. Most of us are familiar with the likable life-of-the-party fellow who makes a joke of everything until the alcohol gives out and the limp laughter is replaced by rivers of tears. For the blocked aspect of the fool it is much the same. The hypocritical mask of levity may hide the fact that this person is feeding on sorrow to the point of gluttony, eating himself or herself alive quite greedily. In order to hide an exaggerated sorrow which says "All is lost!" this person may put on a pitiful show. But in the end the mask cracks from too many tears beneath. The other possibility is that no deception will be attempted. The person will openly wallow in sorrow and stubbornly refuse to release pain or to sacrifice suffering in the service of more life. The blind fool turns away from life altogether.

The alternative to this is a kind of innocent acceptance of the sorrow of loss. The seeing fool is not ashamed to show the sadness of the heart, because what the heart loves is valid, and when the heart loses, sadness is valid. Instead of extraverting sadness in hypocritical or exaggerated behavior, the genuine sorrow of the situation is owned. By honestly experiencing sadness and sorrow over loss, this innocent fool sees a way of returning to life; the sorrow is grounded in reality and connected with the person's whole experience. To describe the beauty of this final reconciliation with reality and with one's self, I can only recall the words spoken to Rachel, weeping over her lost children. God said to her, "Your children will come back to you from the land of the enemy; there is hope for your future."

* * * * *

It is not always clear where the lines are drawn between these grieving styles, or between their negative and positive aspects. Perhaps there are no lines, but a kind of blurring, swirling movement of change and exchange among them. It's not easy to recognize exactly when the mock hero becomes the real hero, the mock martyr becomes the literal martyr-witness, the destructive crazyperson becomes the constructive crazyperson, or the blind fool becomes the seeing fool. All of these possibilities, and any combination of them, exist inside each of us upon confronting painful loss. Sometimes one style may be used to hide another which is more authentic — and more frightening. A client once came to me to deal with anger. We were both surprised when we found that just below consciousness it was not anger that wanted to be expressed, but a deeper and more frightening sorrow. She could act crazy by showing anger and thus never make a fool of herself by being sad. We are sometimes amazingly skilled at unconscious self-protection.

All of the negative aspects of these grieving styles are ways of avoiding the pain of the reality. The mock hero pretends that there is no pain. The negative aspects of the others substitute or exaggerate a secondary pain in order to avoid dealing with the primary pain at the heart of the issue. These negative aspects should not be judged too harshly. We all need to avoid pain until we are ready to bear it. Self-deception is sometimes necessary for survival.

When a person is ready to experience the loss, the positive aspects of these styles emerge. The hero has the courage to face feelings and to meet fear with trust. The martyr-witness has the ability to see the situation realistically and to identify responsibilities accurately. The constructive crazyperson has the ability to express anger accurately and effectively. The innocent and seeing fool has the ability to realize loss and its meaning, and through self-acceptance the fool learns to feel and express compassion for self and for others.

Five

Life Is Goodbye/Life Is Hello*

One More Time

On warm May midnights
under a sinking penumbra,
onthrust of planets and
meteoric lights on the lake,
we walk,

foreshadowing ages of partings
by gun, plane, knife, or sight,
car or water or still imagination.
Not now.

One more time, again, again, again
to lie still by a flame at dawn together.
The window's edge is gilt with sun
dancing like childlike tears through rain.
In other seasons, deep snow for long sleep.

Home is where we never get to
and are always going.
Is it by sea? by train?
by hope? by depths of unfulfillment?

Our last word we never heard,
you and I, whispered in the overflow
of leaving, held close in a little dying
by the timeless caress of joy.

*Goodbye means "God be with you." Hello means "Hail — be well, be whole."

Death in Grief: Disintegration

Grieving for any painful loss means going through a little death. In time, one comes out the other side, a bit worn, perhaps, but in many ways brand new. Like all of nature, we experience many deaths and rebirths throughout our lives. The experience of grieving is one of them. Part of the process of grieving is the pain and bleeding of disintegration which must take place before reintegration can come about.

The Pain

Death in grief is a form of disintegration. Things fall apart. When you go through this death-in-grief, the living functions that keep you together as a living person all fall apart. The little deaths we have to live through before our final death are a series of disintegrations and reintegrations, of dying and being reborn. The dying usually begins in pain.

Falling apart can be a gentle or a violent experience. It can create a sensation of mild loosening and letting go or of violent shattering and sundering of one's being. When dying has a pulling-apart effect, a person often has a sense of impending destruction, as if one's private world were about to end. And in grievous loss, things change; one's small world does end, to yield to a new and changed personal world. This may feel devastating and cataclysmic. Or it may feel quietly inevitable. It may be from a just or an unjust cause. One may feel betrayed, or saved. But letting go of what had been remains painful.

Sometimes the pain can seem so great that a person identifies with it: "I *am* the pain. I am living pain. I embody pain. It is me. I am it. Nothing besides my pain exists for me." This intense experience of pain does not last long. No one could bear it for long. It soon passes into the second sign of woundedness — bleeding.

The Bleeding

In this phase of the dying-that-is-grief, one may have the sense of losing one's self, of spilling out — a kind of bleeding. This usually comes with a feeling of senselessness and meaninglessness; both sense and meaning are lost, along with some of the pain.

They seem to flow out like salt down an hour glass. In "bleeding," one may feel that he or she has nothing to offer anyone: "I am empty, an open wound. A space, a vacuum, a hole is growing inside me taking the place of my self. I am utterly useless." In such an extreme experience of emotional bleeding, a person may now identify with the wound itself: "I am the wound; my wound and I are one."

In both the pain and the bleeding, a person is completely absorbed in the experience of loss, and self-absorbed in the loss of self. The sufferer may think about it all day and dream about it all night. There is little relief. The only safety is in a kind of self-cocooning. Like the chrysalis in the death-phase, the sufferer may wrap himself/herself in a protective membrane and wait.

What one waits for will come.

Rebirth out of Grief: Reintegration

In falling apart and feeling the dying in one's self, because there is little else besides the painful wound to be conscious of, a grieving person tends to be possessive of the pain. In identifying with the pain, the person claims a right to the pain, possesses it: "This is *my* pain. *My* loss. *My* wound." The beginning of rebirth comes when the person is willing to let go of the pain, to become something other than the wound, to grow out of the hurt.

Like the growing chrysalis in its thin elastic sac, the human spirit will expand as it heals until it is ready to burst out of its own self-formed container. For a time, it must be safely contained to go through necessary changes. But as those changes occur, the feeling life of a human being can no longer be contained; it will again enable the person to stretch, to reach, to move, to be. Fullness of being is restored. A new reintegration takes place.

The Dance

This coming forth from the cocoon is a powerful movement. It is like a dance — the dance of new life. A person creates her or his unique dance by releasing powerful feelings safely. This happens by active self-expression through talking and story-telling; through ritualizing, in order to let go of the pain of being separated from one's self and what one loves, and to celebrate reunion; and through the merciful gifts of tears and laughter.

The beautifully expressive model for cocoon-bursting is Nikos Kazantzakis's *Zorba the Greek.* Do you remember the scenes when Zorba meets his misfortunes with a dance? The dance is no light distraction; it embodies grief, pain, despair, and the coexisting energy and determination to live, to remain open to love, to be able to weep and rejoice. Zorba heals himself through the dance.

The Healing

Yes, finally the healing. Coming together. Being one's self again — different from before, older, wiser, more rugged and more sensitive at the same time.

Our faces, like fine crystal, shimmer with interest and design. Each line is an etching of distinct experience honed into the skin as meaning is honed into the soul. Each silver hair on our heads is a moon-gift from God showing the secret night wisdom of suffering borne with love. The gifts of age are symbolic of the changes that give us our unique qualities.

We may feel older before we begin to feel wiser, but remember the lesson of the phoenix who recreates a self from cooling ashes, or the lesson of the salamander who actually lives in fire. So we rise out of our own wounds. So we show wholeness with a kind of luminous transparency through all the burning cracks.

If the wound has been deep, the feeling of wholeness comes only gradually.

Through all the pain and bleeding you have endured, at times you were unable to recognize self-destructive behavior in yourself. But your friends could see more

clearly than you. You paid attention to their observations and listened to their care, and you responded. You came through, for them and for yourself. When you came to the point where you were willing to let go of your pain, to give it up, you may have noticed a change. The pain was still there, but it no longer had the power to hurt you (yes, a contradiction, but you will see what I mean). From then on you began to bear the pain without being diminished or harmed by it. Your anxiety about the pain became reduced. You no longer worried or feared that you would be overcome by the pain, absorbed or consumed by it. It was no longer in charge of you. You were in charge again.

Now the pain was truly yours; you no longer belonged to it or were possessed by it. You owned it and controlled it as your own. There was once again more to life than the pain, since you no longer identified solely with it. You knew, then, that it could not blot you out. It could not kill you or annihilate you. You would survive. All the torn and shredded parts of you began to come together. Sometimes you would pull them together and sometimes they pulled themselves — and you — together. You became yourself again. And you knew that you did this of your own power, and by the grace of life itself. You learned to be grateful again, grateful for life, and grateful to life for calling and pulling you back.

All of this happens because life is goodbye. Life is change. Life means having and holding, then letting go and giving up, even what one loves most, even, eventually, one's own life. But this, you think, would be easier than giving up what you have had to give up

— so much, perhaps, so much more than you will ever be able to tell. But you know what it has all meant to you. You know and God knows, and perhaps one or two others know. You have survived. You can live again. Your life is again your own. And life is also hello. Now you are ready to meet the new, to change with the times, to receive new and different gifts into your life.

You have survived, and soon you will thrive.

Do not worry or be frightened if an aftershock occurs — if after all this, five or twenty years from now, you have disturbing thoughts or dreams of the same old loss. You will be a different person in five or twenty years, and that person may have to face this same old loss on new terms. But it won't take as long or be as difficult. You will have experience and faith to help you. It can make you grow even more, make you even better than before. The pattern is not that of a closed circle which you must repeat again and again, but an open spiral, moving ever outward and inward, returning ever anew to the same points of meaning, ever expanding outwardly from them.

Even old losses never before faced can be healed and absorbed, as long as life and faculties are left — perhaps even without the latter — in God's own mysterious way with the human soul. One of my dear clients knew that she was finally ready to be healed and resolved to struggle through her resistances and face her mother's death of twenty-eight years before. She did so with great courage and determination in only four sessions. By allowing herself to break down and feel the bitter grief and abandonment, the rage and sorrow of that most important loss, she came to break through into a new relationship with her mother as she experiences her to be now, healed from all the separating sins of the past, an active member of the communion of saints. This became more than a comforting doctrine of this woman's faith; it became a reality felt in her life. It is never too late.

Birth Is a Movable Feast

"White is the worst,"
said the midwife.
"Blue and purple are bad
but white means a long time
without oxygen."

I was taken up by alien hands
on Ascension Day, May 15, 1947;
I was denied the long descent down
the birth canal, the first
necessary transit.

Picked like an onion
coiled in the womb
at a time not mine.

No cry. No natural struggle
to be born.

I believe I should have liked
to sleep a bit longer
and would have leapt up singing
later in the day.

So. This primal loss,
the grief of a lifetime,
the quest to be born.

Again and again I struggle
to finish the fear, to swim
into the future, to remember
how it's supposed to be done.

Give me my birthright!
Every day is a happy birthday,
deathday, something-new-to-discover
day. Don't do it for me!
It's my fight, my rite.

In poems, in love, in work:
I will be midwife and mother,
will be the beloved other,
urging.

I will strike, shout, inhale
all life in one swallow,
will sneeze eyeswide, let out
the full blast of delight
in at last achieving delivery.

My hands, blood-covered
in their eager love, croon on:
it's never too late to be born.

Six

Death

Scars

Grieving is an art
like surgery or verse,
essentially the art of healing
loss or losses unaccounted for.

Losses cut the soul
in twos and threes
a wide green gash
like the wound of
a tree cut down
suddenly.

So much more time
than expected
so slowly heals
the severed pieces
of the self shock-shattered
by guilt and rage
and the simple loneliness
of something missing,

the hug, the casual telephone talk,
the good occasional fight lost forever
to the harsh nonphysical world of death.

Grief lived faithfully heals itself
in time not fully.
Where once an open wound burned unbearably
now a thin transparent scar.

Still I know that till
the hour of my own death
the scar glows
and now and then bad weather
will come and waken the same old ache.
A scar is a now and then throb
that dies only with one's own death.

Death is the ultimate reality of loss. Physical death symbolizes all other forms of loss. The way we respond to the physical death of a loved one resembles the way we respond to all the painful losses of our lives. We grieve for all of these. The grieving heals us, though the loss remains. We become able to take the loss back into our lives, to make the reality of it a meaningful part of ourselves. In this way we learn that life contains death, and death gives meaning to life.

In this and the following chapters, we will consider the nature and meaning of specific losses, beginning with physical death as the ultimate loss and the dramatic symbol of all other losses.

Loss of a Link with Life

Probably the most traumatic death anyone has to face is the death of a child or a parent. We not only lose the physical reality of a beloved person. We also lose an important link with life itself: the essential, innocent bond between biological parent and child is broken.

I have never had to face the death of a child, though my heart has yearned over close friends whom I have watched undergo this cruelest loss. The suffering of a powerless child, whose understanding of suffering is limited by few years and small experience, is almost as unbearable to see as the death of a child. When death comes to a child, how terrible the break is for those who are left with their helplessness and defeat! How great the rage must be for a loved one so quickly given and taken! The loss can be life-shattering.

Besides the loss of a much-loved human presence, we feel another kind of loss within ourselves. Through our children, we can feel again the happiness of our own childhoods — from which we had been cut off at age thirteen or eighteen or twenty-one. We are again magically empowered with the secret dreams and longings of the seemingly eternal world of the young. When we lose a loved child, especially a younger child or an only child, we are once again — much more cruelly than before — banished from this wonderful realm.

So we grieve over the loss of one of the most blessed gifts of all — the gift of accompanying a young person on his or her discovery of life. In a secondary way, we also grieve over the sobering change in ourselves. We have lost a part of ourselves and the joy we had found as parents of that child, along with the youthful exuberance, fresh view of life, and sense of wonder which our children can inspire in us.

It is not much easier for a child to lose a parent, though if the child is fully grown, the harsh unfairness of the loss is less burdensome. For a child, even a grown-up child functioning as an independent and competent adult, a parent always symbolizes the deepest longing for security and comfort. A parent means home. Because of the special biological bond we have with our mothers, our own bodies carry an image of Mother that means our own deepest sense of life. The loss of either parent, but especially of a mother, means the loss of one's own connectedness with life, with the wholeness of creation. Of course, the connection is not broken with a parent's death, but our sense of it may be clouded for a time. We may lose the comforting sense of ourselves as innocent creatures who are children of the universe, who have a right to be here.

When my own mother died, I lost the awareness of myself as a proper part of the universe, a fellow creature in a wondrous creation. Beyond the personal sense of loss of my mother as a particular woman whom I loved, I felt disconnected with the planet in some way. This uneasy feeling lasted from the moments after her death until her burial. I was with my mother when she died, and I was keenly aware of the tremendous privilege of witnessing such a major transition in her life. It was as if I were the midwife, honored to help my mother give birth to herself into a new and unimaginable state. It was her birthday into Paradise, and I was permitted to be present. A second before her last breath, I had an image of three people: I was walking, with a newborn baby in my arms, up to a gate through which I knew I could not pass. From the other side of the gate, another woman was walking toward me with her arms outstretched; it was my grandmother, my mother's mother. We met at the gate, and I delivered the baby into her arms. We smiled, bowed, and it was over.

After my mother's funeral in the tiny Russian church where I had been baptized twenty-five years earlier, I accompanied her body to Canada to be buried next to her own mother's body. I was already ordained then, so I officiated at my mother's burial myself, which seemed so much more appropriate to me than any other arrangement. I held the daughter-rites for her burial. As I poured earth over her body I regained my sense of belonging to the earth myself, of being a natural child of this planet, physically and spiritually one with all creation.

Suddenly the words I had read so often in the Gospel became real: "Unless a grain of wheat falls into the ground and dies it abides alone; but if it dies, it brings forth much fruit." I had an image of a tiny, shriveled pine seed placed side by side with a fully mature and magnificent pine tree. Someone who had newly arrived from Jupiter or Mars would have no way of looking at the two things and knowing that they were one and the same, so different would they appear.

And so it was with my mother's body as I knew it, and as I was now committing it into the good ground, like a small seed. I had no way of imagining what her new being was like, though I knew and felt it to be alive in some way and connected with this familiar body I had known and loved and come from. I understood in my soul and in my bones for the first time what the Christian church meant by "the resurrection of the body and the life of the world to come." I didn't believe — I *knew*. And I *belonged*. The process and inexpressible mystery of life and death, physicality and spirituality, included me. Through experiencing my mother's death I both lost and regained my sense of creaturely innocence.

Daughter-rite

I sang at my mother's deathbed
and stood to honor the dream
of her life, pure and complete
(her name means Essence),
to honor the gift of the dream
passed on to me,
to receive the daughter-right,
her name;
then held my breath
and courted her death
with a vision of dancers,
a great invisible orchestra,
and pink roses;
courted my mother's death
and gave back breath
and became midwife
for her birthday into Paradise.

A year later I wrote this peaceful poem:

After a Year, Only Bones

Bones are long and narrow,
longer and narrower than flesh,
which is wide and warm.

My mother's bones
are long and narrow
and rooted in the ground,
a strong tree growing
inward, or upside down.

Loss of Intimacy

When we lose a loved one to physical death, we lose a sense of belonging. We need to feel that we belong here, and that we have a vital part in life as it unfolds. We belong in our own lives, and we belong in other people's lives as we touch. Each of us has a need and a right to enjoy intimacy with others. How painful is this loss of closeness, rightness, and belonging when an intimate physical bond with another being is broken. The nature and depth of the loss depend on the nature and depth of the bond. We can feel it with a friend, a spouse or lover, a child, a place, a pet or other fellow creatures. My whole neighborhood is grieving right now over the loss of a beautiful, stately old tree that was blown down in the back yard next door during a storm last month.

We feel cheated and violated, for we all enjoyed the particular relationship we had with the admirable and ancient tree. No one owned it, but we all belonged to it. In a sense, we have been orphaned, and we need to comfort each other.

Lovers and spouses share a particular intimacy that is violated by physical death. Sometimes the violation occurs long before actual biological death, as in the case of prolonged illness that separates one mate from the other and breaks the flow of intimacy between them.

A recent Canadian study shows that surviving spouses of persons killed by cancer have an intensely difficult grief process, more so than persons widowed by heart disease, for example. The study indicates that this is because in most cases studied, the possibility of the spouse's death was never discussed by the couple; because the physical side of the disease is looked on by society as particularly ugly, an onus which does not encourage the maintenance of physical intimacy; and because the surviving spouses did not see themselves as essential parts of the final days of their mates' lives, since there was little they could actively do to help gain control over the disease.

Fortunately, this situation is rapidly changing. We are more educated and sensitive as a culture to the nature of this illness, more open and free to share our feelings concerning death, more open about the process of dying. Indeed, with cancer and other debilitating diseases, much of the family's and friends' grieving can be shared openly with the afflicted person before death.

Dr. Elisabeth Kubler-Ross's identification of the five common emotional responses to the knowledge of one's own imminent death — denial, anger, bargaining, depression, and acceptance — has been useful therapeutically for the dying and the bereaved. The tremendous work of the Hospice Movement throughout the world has helped thousands face their own deaths or the deaths of loved ones with great openness and loving integrity. Groups such as Make Every Day Count and I Can Cope have given open support to persons with terminal cancer. Psychic healing through meditation and visualization has given persons with chronic illnesses greater power in their own physical or spiritual healing — whether the form of healing is in physical recovery or a good death. Consciousness-raising plays such as *The Shadow Box* by Michael Cristofer have helped us deal honestly with our fears when confronted with fatal illness. There is increasing help for the spouses of those who are about to die, and it is important for all of us to become informed of these resources and to use them.

When one's mate is physically violated by disease, sometimes it is impossible not to feel violated oneself. It is more than the death of a lover that causes grief — it is the insult and injury of the dying: We regret not only the death, but even more the dying.

When two people are deeply in love and are physically and spiritually one with each other, the physical death of one of them can mean a spiritual death for the other, as this love poem reveals:

You are my body
and I am yours;
we have no home
except inside each other.

When you are away from me
my whole body is amputated from itself,
and I am homeless.

Through a prolonged dying there is violation; but when a loved one is yanked away from us suddenly, without warning, it is a kind of amputation of the soul which must be endured. Even such enormous wounds heal, though the loss remains and is real. In either case, there is no choice but to work through one's pain, to *remember* the joyous gifts of life, and to wait. Wait as long as it takes. Healing comes, both to those stricken and to those who grieve. In serious illness, healing may take the form of physical recovery, or of death, the ultimate healing. In grief, healing helps us make peace with the meaning of death, which cannot be understood except as an unknown part of life.

Death of a Dream

We all know what it is to lose oneself to a dream. And when the dream is lost, that part of ourselves we invested in the dream also seems lost to us. The dream is broken, and something inside breaks too. The dream could be for so many things — or for one very special thing. A secret wish for ourselves. A private longing. A hope we may always hold sacred. How especially bitter is the death of a special dream. How betrayed we feel by a dream that shaped us and now leaves us stranded in the wake of its failure. Perhaps it was always nothing more than illusion. Perhaps it never had a chance. Our goal was too lofty. We had an unrealistic notion of life, of ourselves, of a special someone who was not after all what we had imagined. No matter. How it hurts to let this one go, to give up a dream!

I believe we can only live by keeping our dreams alive, and if one dream dies, we must search down inside for the seeds of another. Not all dreams are based on illusions. Every lovely reality was once someone's dream that was loved or longed into being. You yourself may exist because you were once someone's dream. We all may have been spun into life because God dreamed us so vividly and loved us so much we were simply yearned into material being. We owe our dreams everything. When they die, we owe them recognition and acknowledgment in their passing.

Political Grief

Dreams transcend the personal. They exist in the realm of principle and ideal, in the political as well as the private sphere. The domain of public principles is expressed through the political life of a people. Conflicts within that shared arena inevitably end in rejoicing for some, grieving for others. When one's sense of justice has been violated, one's hopes deferred for the future of a community when an issue fails or a trusted candidate loses, when the cause of equality is postponed, there is bound to be the chaos, confusion, and a feeling of impotence over a dream that's gotten kicked around and tumbled dead into a corner.

Collective Grief

Political grief is collective grief, the shared grief of a community united in principle or ideal. When a living symbol or hero of that unity is attacked or killed, we will be publicly grieved, enraged by a violation of the values that bind us. Can we ever forget the collective and publicly shared grief expressed in our own lifetime for the Kennedy brothers and Martin Luther King in this country, and for symbolic and heroic leaders like Steve Biko in struggling South Africa? We suffer such great losses not only in isolation, but in the strength of our human solidarity.

Death Is Being Left

The chief brutality of physical death is that someone is left. There is a dreadful, foul, nasty feeling in being abandoned. The parting was not mutual. One person went away. The other stayed. Neither one, perhaps, out of choice. Death rarely allows for elegant departures and tidy farewells. It comes between people randomly. Someone is left with the anguish of having been left unilaterally and unfairly. The leaving is not so bad when there is an agreed understanding beforehand, when there is time and space for a good goodbye. It's when there was no goodbye, or worse, a bad goodbye, that death becomes hateful, leaving one with a feeling of incompletion and irresolution, with no more chance of completing or resolving the relationship which is cut in that final way.

But perhaps there is a chance. I can do something very tangible and write you a letter, something that I myself can touch and see and hold. I can read it out loud to you. I can feel your response. I can even hear you dictating a letter back to me, and write it down for you, to give to myself and to keep as a reminder of this healing conversation. You give me good to keep, you who have left me.

One can, after all, do what is necessary within one's self. And the image of the one who has gone still exists inside me. It is up to me, now, to struggle through and make the relationship come as right as possible. I will not be defeated by this death, pulled into a pit of living death because of it — not for long. I know now what I must do. Find you within me, you who have died and left me, and face you and your leaving, and hold you with me long enough, this time, to say my own goodbye to you in my own way, taking as long as I need to take.

And this I will do. In order to be free of your ghost. In order to be free to meet you in whatever new reality may be in store for us. I will finally make myself say goodbye to you, and I will not just helplessly watch you leave this time. I will bless you and say "Go," and I will send your ghost away from me with love or anger or whatever is right between us. If death has robbed me of my power in our relationship, I will take back that power. And you and I will part in peace.

A Note on the Communion of Saints

You may or may not share my bias of belief in life after death and in the ongoing possibility of soul-to-soul communication — one of the Christian creeds calls this the "communion of saints." If you do, I encourage you to act on your faith by cultivating a new relationship with important and loved people in your life who have died. This relationship need no longer be bound by the separating sins (brokenness, alienation) of the past, or the limitations of time and space. On the night of my mother's death as I was weeping, I suddenly sensed her presence; I *felt* her with me as a lovely, robust young woman. The message seemed to be "You can't imagine what it's like for me now. It's *as if* God had made me young again, forever. It is like a new learning — exciting. Grieve now. And when you are done, remember that I am here, waiting, and always with you." So I hurt and mourned for three years, but I remembered. And I am now enjoying a growing new relationship with a person who loved me and gave me life.

Midwives

1.

The mother dreams outloud between
the falling of an eyelid between
waves of the ocean between
the arms of one daughter and the other.

She dreams her choices in timeless light.

The choice of the chrysalis
to unfold into wings
to take flight or not
to stay tight and wither slowly
on the dry bark of an old tree
or to blow itself into space
on a cloud of gold
and if so, to speed north or south
and in time for what awakening
and in whose vision of living or dying
and out of whose dreamspun sleep?

The choice of silence to become
not only sound but splendor
in a rush of music
in a leap of breath
in a body of wood or bones
and if so, what body and where
and inside whose bones
will she burst into song?

The choice of the mother lode
to let itself be found, be overheard
in its river-rush beneath all surfaces
so hidden, crimson, flooding with gold
the veins and creases of daughter-soil
rich, rich beyond bearing, beyond comprehension.

She dreams.

2.

The wishes of the daughters
toward the beloved mother-tree
are felt, not seen, by faces, not eyes,
known in the hands which hover over
the vines of the body their shoots
uprooted from — wishes, wishes
to give back to the tree the gift
of flowing green, all the tree green
in the world, all the truest green
of deep down living things
contained so well in the familiar,
the well-known stranger, this womanroot
which gave them birth.

The daughters listen
and their four ears become nightflowers
tuned to the hum of the dreaming moon,
their mother.

She speaks in language plucked from strings so far past,
from time immemorial, yet memorable inside their
shared secrets of sisterspeech:

their language is history and their mother
a floating historian set free in time,
divining her own spaces for miracles,
events, jokes, bizarre lines they must catch
in cold air as they fall free,
take dreaming-time to find —

unimagined, nonsensical, too clear, too sharp,
too full of perfect sense and image.

Flowing branches of her riverbed
the three are led down known ways into the unknown,
each invoking a different myth with the same tongue,
separate, melting, a sparkle of threes into one.

She knows and they hear.
She knows more than she knows
and they hear more than they hear.

The daughter-rivers hold holy water.
She the drink, they the drinkers,
drifting in her mother-sun.

They hear her dreaming,
    bathe the dreamer with their love.

3.

The mother's body, itself an egg
cracking, spilling — but out of which no known
can come.
                Will heaven be born
or earth regained from its brittle opening?

The women wait
for the coming forth,
praying to be worthy
to hear the new voice
and strong to bear its cry.

The daughters and mother wait
as sisters in the service of birth,
trusting the surprise, the stretching
of their souls into giddy grief
and breathless hope:

for reunion, for soft unhurried singing
for constant, trustworthy daylight
for easy, protective night
for casualness and mere conversation
for the very ordinariness of daily life
for being able to take things for granted.

Longing and waiting, waiting and yearning
through a triune vigil of dreams.

4.

From the depths of your long awaiting
from deprivation of the common

     from the milk of your devotion
     from the oceans of your care

          Life will go on.

From the breast of the living God
          Life will be borne.

Dance for Me When I Die

A woman ran through a tunnel toward the ocean
  and she danced, she danced in the ocean.
A woman ran through a tunnel toward her death
  and they danced, they danced for her death.

Nobody's grandmother
I'll be a fairy
godmother if you
choose me

How I'd love to be
around with roses
when you ring forth
in glory

So make a promise
wish for wish —
I'll sing to all
your rainbow living

If you will laugh
once, weep a little,
and dance for me
when I die.

Love Mantra for Letting Go

I bless you
I release you

I set you free
I set me free

I let you be
I let me be

Seven

Birth and Parenting

Birth: The Primal Angst*

In the beginning being without breath,
change or loss of breath, choking;
squeezed from gills into lungs
the baby screams, the infant swims in air,
betrayed by the body, divided
in brutal duality, passing from one into two,
from amniotic unity to I and not-I,
Mother and Self,
from breathing through skin
to breathing thin air,
first defeated by the first despair
making us Other in an alien world.

The original violence shared by all,
the choking in the narrows,
the scream in the hands of a stranger.

To survive is triumph,
to wake into cold life
from the eternal sleep
of the innocent body,

only to sleep our loss anew
and dream again of the longed-for warmth
in the memory of our mother's mandala womb.

*Angst: The rite of passage; "a choking in the narrows."

It is painful to be left, and it is also painful to take one's leave, as we all do when we leave the womb in birth, and when we leave the body in death. To take leave of one's self, one's senses, one's life, one's loves as one knew them. In this, birth and death are the same. As every death is a form of rebirth into a beyond which we can't now imagine, every birth is a form of dying — of separation from the miraculous world of the womb where everything was once blissfully provided.

Not every mother, child, and family experiences a new birth in exactly the same way. Not every pregnancy or delivery is the same. Some women have delightful pregnancies with never a moment's doubt or disturbance. Some women never have a trace of anxiety about giving birth. Some families have beautiful transitions in accommodating the new member. Some babies are born with ease. But I very much doubt that every woman, child, and family goes through the experience of pregnancy and birth without some stress, and for many, this stress can be of a grievous nature. Through this wonderful process, new life takes its place. And there is a displacement of things, in order to make a new space. In some cases, the displacement can be painful. It is helpful to recognize this possibility, and to meet it with the assurance that you are not alone, that there is nothing bad or wrong in feeling as you do.

Loss of Physical Self-image in Pregnancy

To lose your familiar shape, to look in the mirror and see your body taking strange, unfamiliar proportions and curves — this can be a traumatic experience. Who is that? It can't be me! All of the dramatic physiological changes that a woman goes through in her pregnancy can be image-shattering. Many women will meet these changes with ambivalence: on the one hand, "How thrilling that a new life is being formed inside me, actually visible in its progress through the change in my outward shape"; on the other hand, "Good grief — I'll never be the same again!" Joy and despair, one after the other, or both at the same time! And this confusion is not helped by the hormonal changes that are going on inside. So much to feel. So long to wait. My body a stranger to itself. Invaded. Stretched. I may feel better than I ever have or will again in my whole life, and I may look healthier, too. Or I may feel and look awful.

Wait. In a long and a short time, you will be able to recognize yourself again. The security in your own body that you have lost will come back to you. And you may even be glad for the experience — at least, for the amazing gift that has come from it. But for now, if you feel bad, that's all right. Give yourself twice as much love and attention — not just for the baby, but because your body is doing a double job and you deserve to be treated like a queen during these months. Go ahead and grieve over the lost princess figure you once had, over the dependable emotions you can no longer count on, and over the favorite sports you may have to give up for now. Your reward will be with you soon, and for a long time.

Loss of Freedom and Privacy

The whole family has to adjust to making room for the new member. This means room in both space and time.

123

For parents who have been alone together, the enjoyment of privacy and the freedom to go places on the spur of the moment may be much more limited than before. A friend of mine in her ninth month of her first pregnancy wailed to her spouse one night, "John, do you realize we'll never be *alone together* again?" Now that their son has been with them for a few months, they have actually managed to find occasional moments of privacy, and they realize that their social life did not come to an end, though they are experiencing some limitations.

Loss of Self-confidence

Nothing can make two intelligent, competent adults feel more clumsy and inadequate than the arrival of a dependent baby. A woman or man who is normally very self-confident and capable becomes a parent and suddenly questions whether anything she or he does is right. Worry, worry, worry. Loss of peace of mind, along with a lot of sleep for the first few weeks! But as time goes by, both sleep and peace will be restored.

Loss of Security in Childbirth

The dreams of a pregnant woman are sometimes haunted by the insecurity of the unknown: imagined dangers of childbirth, both for herself and the child; the possibility of birth defects over which she will have no control whatever; the distance that may come between her and her spouse, her other children, her friends and career, when this child is born; her loss of "normalcy" during pregnancy and afterwards. The loss of emotional security can affect both parents during this time. I know mothers with outrageously healthy children who had nightmares of giving birth to monsters before each child was born. Such helpless anxiety is the fruit of lost security in the face of the unknown.

Then there are the sorrowful realities of dangers come true. Only today a woman shared with me the story of her second daughter's birth thirty years ago and of how the birth has deeply affected her whole life. When my friend was nineteen, she lost her first child through miscarriage. She immediately became pregnant again, but suffered a serious fall near the time of delivery and was deprived the natural birth she had hoped for when her daughter was taken by Caesarean section. She became pregnant for the third time and enjoyed an easy pregnancy. Because of last minute medical complications, she was again deprived of a natural delivery and underwent a second C-section at 7:30 in the evening.

When she awakened in her hospital room hours later and asked for her baby, she was told the baby was sleeping and could not be brought to her. Throughout the night and the next morning she continued to ask for her child and was told the same story. She did not believe the nurses. She was by now convinced that the child was dead. By late morning, her pediatrician walked into the room and casually said, "Oh, have they told you your child is deformed?" A triple shock: "My baby is *not* dead. My baby is *alive*. My baby is *deformed*." He left her with her confusion. When the baby was finally brought to her, she examined her carefully. Since the shock had primed her to expect the worst, she was by then relieved to see that only her daughter's right hand, leg, and foot were affected — her leg being nearly severed by a tight band of skin cutting through the calf.

For the next three days in her hospital bed, my friend thought these things: "What happened? What did I do wrong or what did I not do? Was it my fault? What happened in the delivery room?"

On the fourth or fifth day, this changed. She became aware of a presence, and this presence conveyed a message to her: "What matters now is only that she is your child, and that it has been given to you to be with her in life, to help her in any way you can, and to realize that your life and her life have a purpose which it is for you to accomplish together." From then on, this woman knew and understood that her task was to do all she could for her daughter medically, but beyond that, to help her know her own worth, dignity, and capability as a human being. Today, the daughter has two children of her own. She skis, skates, and has enjoyed performing in the ballet. The guiding presence never left her or her mother. I believe it is a presence that lives within each of us; we have only to open ourselves to it in times of grievous loss to find a source of fullness and possibility within the human spirit.

Loss of Physical Union

When two beings — mother and child — have experienced such physical closeness for so long, birth is a traumatic separation for both of them. If we could remember being born, we might recall a kind of animal terror in being helplessly propelled out of the safe warmth of a mother's body. The trauma exists for both mother and child.

The mother must recognize the child as a truly separate being from herself. In naming a child, she acknowledges that it is a distinct person, an individual, and her genetic bond with this new person is only a small part of what will determine who the child will become. If we look on our children as extensions of ourselves, we deny each child's uniqueness, the miracle of individuality. If the child is regarded as a possession with whom we can do what we will, this violates a human being's birthright to be her or his own person. The child is someone outside his or her parents' reality — part of it, but beyond it. A child belongs to the future once he or she is actually born into the physical world. A child's potential exists in the child's otherness.

The awesome process of watching a person grow can only come with the recognition that, once born, this new being is no longer merely a part of the mother's body or the family tree. Someone new has come into the world in a unique package. A mother must let go, in a biological sense, in birth, though nursing can be a gentle way of physically releasing her child from her body.

Other Losses in Parenting

Both parents must spend their lives learning the infinitely difficult art of holding their children close with open arms — the balance of necessary nurturing, and necessary letting go — one of the hardest tasks I know.

The physical cord is cut at birth, but the emotional cord gets gnawed inelegantly away through the child's growing years, most painfully for parents and children both during adolescence. When the child finally leaves home for good, the emotional umbilical cord of the old bond is finally severed, and the relationship undergoes change from protective parent/dependent child to adult/ adult. When the gnawing ends and parents and adult children can stand face to face, they may discover people whom they can respect, like, and enjoy. Meanwhile, both need all the help and support they can get.

Other more desolate losses connected with parenting have to do with a separation for which there is no consolation: the loss of life in miscarriage. There is no more possibility for the special direction that specific life might have taken. Other children may come, but that makes this particular loss no less real. Also, a woman's body may take longer to recover from miscarriage, or from the death of a child at birth, than from normal pregnancy and delivery. A mother has had to endure the difficult changes of pregnancy without the joyous reward of a new child to help establish a new normalcy, and the body feels this as keenly as the heart.

Even when a woman makes a clear decision to terminate an unwanted or dangerous pregnancy by abortion, she needs to say goodbye to the particular possibility of that new life and to recognize that seldom is the relief of such a decision unmitigated by a sense of loss and some sorrow.

Women and men who experience infertility when

they desire children must also undergo a redefinition of themselves. They may feel alienated from their own bodies which refuse to give them the longed-for children. Through compassion for the limitations of the flesh, they can come to forgive the limits of their own bodies, to be reconciled to themselves. Couples must go through this mutually to avoid the bitterness of blaming the other as well as oneself for what clearly cannot be helped. The way past blame and guilt is in compassion for the other and forgiveness for oneself. Then a new unity may be established, a more authentic home created to welcome homeless children who may not be the body's offspring, but can become true heart's children.

Another way of losing a child in our culture is through loss of custody in a divorce settlement. The parent who has fought to keep the child suffers a universe-shattering loss when that battle is lost. There is little consolation for this felt injustice, other than to remind oneself over and over that the loss need not be permanent. Physical separation is temporary, and as the child grows, emotional distances may diminish. One holds on to hope when all else is taken.

All of these separations are easier to bear with the support of family and friends. Without help or understanding, the new parent, or the redefined parent, is likely to feel confused, inadequate, and abandoned. The feeling might be relieved if one were simply to shout out, "Will someone please help me!" Help may be closer at hand than imagined. Suggestions of the kinds of groups or agencies which offer help are listed under Other Resources on pages 202 and 203.

Eight

Change

Life Does

Creation's pace
ebbs away
little by little
at the old
flesh.

Used to be
brandy
made me high.
Now
it puts me to sleep.

People change.

I could
out-love
anyone
before.

Bones brittle
cinder
pop out.

A soft bed
used to be
heaven.
Now it's a romping
nighthorse.
Life does, doesn't it?

Things change. No one stays the same. Life moves. We move with it or die. But there are natural resistances within us; even organisms born to change fight it. From the safety of sameness, we confront the possibility of change, with fear, tension, then yielding, letting be. We grieve for change, yet we grow through change.

Change in Place

Have you ever sat and cried, disturbed and lonely, in a strange motel room in a strange city, longing for your family, your dog, your own bed? Have you ever had to leave home for good, but it didn't feel good at all? Have you ever watched a house you used to live in get torn down? Or painted an ugly color by new owners? Have you ever moved into a brand new office, much better than your old one, and felt out of place and uneasy? Have you moved the furniture in your living room and felt confused for days, not knowing why, because you really like the new arrangement much better than the way it was before? Have you finally taken the trip to Europe, Martha's Vineyard, or Southern California, delighted with everything you see, but counting the days until you can look at your own front door again?

Places are important. Place is how you define your sense of space — of what is *your* space. You know how you feel in your own space. Life is secure. Your own responses are predictable. But lose the space that means "home" to you, and your whole psychological system may be askew, sometimes much to your surprise or shame. Don't be ashamed. You are like every other

creature of nature. You like to know your own territory, proclaim your own boundaries — if not to the world, at least to yourself. A lot of moving around can upset the system. Your body might let you know how little you like physical changes, even if intellectually you pride yourself on being easy-going and progressive.

Think of all the little secret griefs that accompany every exciting move or trip. Subtle griefs, not ones that you would call out loud by that name. You might think of them as stresses or difficulties in adjustment. But something quietly important to you has been left behind. If it's true that you are feeling some unspecific and illogical sadness, find out what it is about the old places that holds meaning for you. Recognition makes letting go much easier. The new places, after all, might be better, in their own way, given a chance — given new meaning.

Change in Position

Just as change in place causes stress and quiet grief, so do many kinds of changes in position or situation. Some of these are:

Getting married: losing your independence, your sense of being number one all by yourself; losing the privilege of occasional irresponsibility.

Getting a job: losing your identity as a student; losing the freedom to be lazy and play hooky twice a month if you feel like it.

Getting unemployed: losing a job, possibly the sense of worth or self-importance that went with it; losing financial security; losing a familiar routine; losing the contacts you made on the job.

Getting retired: losing your absolute certainty of being useful; losing the appreciation for your work; losing skills; losing the expectancy of physical health that comes with feeling valued and useful.

Marriage. Career. Parenthood, changing as children come and grow and go. Retirement.

Loss. Recognition of loss. Grief. Then getting ready for something new, for doing and being something new.

Change in Person

Other kinds of changes — changes which affect your person — require special attention and care:

Unforeseen accidents: changes in your appearance; radical effects upon your lifestyle; loss of bodily function or of an essential ability.

Diet depression: grieving for loss of weight, loss of food, or favorite foods. The weight *was* me, now it's gone. My own flesh is leaving me. I'm more exposed, vulnerable, having lost my protective bulk of fat.

Sudden and undesired weight gain. Probably even more devastating than weight loss is this physical change and its attendant lowering of self-esteem. This can happen in times of stress. I can choose to use food to medicate my feelings, to protect, or to abuse my body. If I do make this choice, I must remember that I have the power to change again later, to take off the extra weight. I must also remember that it will be difficult and require commitment. Is it worth it? Can I respect and love myself enough now, in stress, not to overeat, but to swim instead, or walk, or do other tension-releasing things for myself? These activities are as comforting as eating is but probably will not harm me, even if I should forget my limits and do them to excess. If my self-worth has gone, getting fat will put off its return. I can help my self-worth return by knowing that it is a pleasure to be slender and self-respecting as much as it is a pleasure to be well-fed and comforted. If I choose the latter, then I need to make a commitment to love myself and respect myself in a new and larger body. I may not use my body weight as an excuse for self-hate!

Self, what other changes make you squirm? What is the vulnerable underside of your human growth? What does time do to you?

Crisis in middle life: loss of satisfaction in what you're doing and who you are; loss of physical or spiritual fertility.

Aging: loss of being able to rely on your body being the same and doing the same for you. Not only does time not always heal wounds, sometimes time *is* the wound.

Visiting the Old Folks' Home

"Old woman, why do I fear you?"
"Child, you are afraid
you will catch my death."

Aging takes us near to eternity, but it is more than waiting to die. Aging is an eternal growing that can deepen us in our being each year we are given.

The art of aging goes like this:
two or three silver hairs caught
sparkling in the sun at twenty-four;
vagrant laugh lines appear at thirty-six;
double dry martinis at forty-two
and an hour earlier to bed at fifty.
Finally what one waited for comes
with such clarity and relief:
the disguise breaks down,
mask of adulthood cracks,
wears out, peels off, and the forty-year deception
of being grown-up crumbles completely
into original childhood's honest joy
somewhere after sixty.
Or a magic zipper allows us in and out at will
all along the way, if we're good.

Change in Consciousness

One of the chief goals of human life is spiritual growth — the training, raising, and deepening of one's consciousness. Creating values. Forming sensitivities. Sharpening perception. Learning appropriate responses. Moving more deeply and effectively in and out of one's self, to improve the quality of human communication and to contribute to the quality of life on the planet.

The gain of consciousness means the loss of *unconsciousness.* The acquisition of knowledge requires the loss of ignorance. Sometimes this loss can be very painful indeed. Opening one's eyes to the painful realities that surround us: poverty, hunger, disease, hideous inhuman cruelties inflicted by humanity on itself; dignity-diminishing sexism, racism, agism, and classism; life-denying hatreds of all sorts and conditions. It is not easy or pleasant to permit oneself to see. I recall a haunting song by Carole Etzler which begins half angrily, "Sometimes I wish my eyes hadn't been opened." Sometimes. But there are other times when to *know* is life-saving, when one realizes that it is *necessary to know* in order to live honestly, with compassion, with appropriate humility — in order to live at all in human terms.

The loss of consciousness may be worse — to forget what has been learned, to shut out reality. This kind of loss is less painful, perhaps, because one is not as alive, not as much a part of the world-building process humankind has undertaken. But the closing off of reality, even by one person, means a greater loss for those who are left to continue.

There is some grief either way, for something is lost when one's way of seeing and knowing changes, for better or worse. Perhaps we learn more quickly and intensely when we are young, because change comes with less depth and density of loss to children with fewer years of attachments behind them.

Children and Change

Children can feel loss very acutely when it happens. What they lack in a sense of accumulative time they make up for in immediacy of experience. If children are helped to deal with loss when it comes to them, they will be spared having to assimilate old hurts when they are of an age when unrealized losses can emerge in destructive ways.

Children think very literally. A sensitive child's grieving can be sharpened by concrete images that give the event of loss a magical power. It is especially important for adults to encourage children to talk about their grief, in order to help them discern reality from the often frightening images and beliefs they can develop.

When a child first confronts the strangeness of death, euphemisms to cloak the reality of it are not only useless, but can be confusing and damaging. With children, who take things so literally, honesty is the best policy. If you tell a child that grandfather is "sleeping" or "with God," the child may wonder why grandfather never seems to waken, and fear that if he or she — the child — falls asleep, this same disaster may occur. The child may equate "being with God" to going to Disneyland or being on the moon or floating in space without meals and company.

It is better to explain that when a person dies, everything stops — there is no breathing, no movement, no conversation, no life — and to demonstrate that this is a natural and essential part of life. Point out how in the winter in many parts of the country trees and flowers die, so that in spring new life can take their place. If the adults have a belief in afterlife, it may be helpful to share that belief with a child, but very carefully, so as not to leave a wrong impression of ghosts or frightening images of reward and punishment. The simpler the explanation, the better. Images may be helpful, but they must be chosen very thoughtfully, since young children will take them literally and concretely.

I have explained to children that we simply don't know what happens after a person dies, just as the leaves can't imagine what will follow them when they fall off a tree. But we know that in the spring, new buds will form on the tree. These don't look like leaves right at first. But soon they grow, and the whole life cycle begins again.

And then I explain that I believe something just as wonderful happens when people die, but we can't imagine it. It will come to each of us, after we've done all we were meant to do the way we are now. It's important for me to emphasize that there is no hurry to find out, since everyone will find out at the end of this life. Some children are so impressed by a naturalistic description of death that they become curious and eager to experience it for themselves!

Concrete minds are very delicate and determined. Adults need to learn that sometimes the best thing to tell children is the truth — that we don't know all the answers. Then of course it may be helpful for the adult and child together to talk about what they hope and imagine will happen to a beloved pet who has died, a relative, or a friend. The subject must be thoroughly talked over — that's important.

A wonderful way of helping resolve a child's loss is suggested in Judith Viorst's book, *The Tenth Good Thing about Barney* *: Name the ten best things you can think of about the person or pet that died. I know of a teacher who used this suggestion with her third grade class when their pet sand crab died. This cheered

*See Helpful Resources, "Grieving and Children," page 198.

everyone up and made the children recall how they had enjoyed their pet, and they were able to *say* how glad they were to have enjoyed it during its lifetime.

When children face loss it is chiefly a matter of facing change — change in attachments. A child becomes attached to a favorite teacher and grieves when the teacher goes away or when the school year comes to an end. A child grieves over moving away from close friends or playmates. Loss is very clearly a detaching process. And in facing this, a child may go through grieving as any adult would, feeling fear, guilt, anger, and sadness.

Fear may manifest itself specifically, as a fear that going to sleep or having an illness (any illness) will cause death; or a fear that moving away from friends means that one will never have friends again. Much reassurance is needed.

Guilt can come out of the belief in one's own magical power. A group of children in a children's home met a new boy with hostility, because he was obnoxious and not very likable. One of the children shouted during a playground argument, "I wish you were dead." By a horrible coincidence, the boy drowned while bathing alone the next day. All of the children felt terrible. Some of them believed the accident was their fault because they had not been very nice to him. You can imagine how the boy felt who had wished him dead.

The sensitive counselors arranged for a memorial service in which each of the children could make a gift representing their wishes for the dead child and say a few words to express how she or he felt. They talked about death being an accident, something unpredictable, and said that the boy who had died was peaceful now, and would never be unhappy again. Most importantly, now he understood how his behavior made the other children feel bad and show mean feelings to him, and he would freely and gladly forgive them. Thanks to caring adults, the children in this situation were allowed to work through their feelings about death in a loving and supportive atmosphere.

Even a very young child can be affected by loss and can act out feelings of guilt and resentment. My friend Pesha's mother died when she was seventeen months old. Her father told her years later that right after her mother's death her behavior changed. She began to climb up into a hard, uncomfortable wooden chair, and she would sit there for hours without moving. As a young adult, Pesha noticed that she would always sit in an uncomfortable chair to read, as if to deliberately deprive herself of the pleasure of reading. In some way, could that little child have felt responsible — even *guilty* — for her mother's going away forever? Could she have encased her small self in resentment as she withdrew on that hard chair to inflict her self-punishment? How easily and how early we believe the worst about ourselves! And how long we cling to our beliefs! How much we need to help each other through the agonies of change and separation, all through our lives.

Chemical Dependency and Change

Just as one's self-image changes and suffers through the abuse of food, the abuse of alcohol or other mood-altering chemicals can cause one of the most severe losses of all — the radical diminishment of self-esteem. The lower self-esteem has fallen, the higher the compensatory bravado may appear in the person who is lost in the despair of alcohol or other drug dependency. Since loss of the sense of self-worth is always the worst symptom of grief, grief is a central reality of chemical dependency.

The pattern of the disease is circular. As self-esteem diminishes, one medicates feelings more and more, increasing the loss of self-esteem. Chronically abused chemicals are at best a pseudo-anesthetic for the psyche; at worst, they are lethal contaminants to the whole system. Ultimately, as the pain of using them becomes greater than the pain of not using them, treatment and recovery can begin.

Of course, the recovery process for the chemically dependent person involves losses, too. Many of these are positive losses — the loss of delusion, of denial, of isolation, of indulgence in self-pity and self-hate.

Other losses during recovery may be truly grievous, involving changes in one's fundamental self-image, life patterns, and relationships. Since the disease of chemical dependency seldom is checked soon enough to avoid all tragic consequences, the recovering chemically dependent person already may have lost his or her job, marriage, family members, friends, or health. Without the anesthetizing chemical, these losses may be felt for the first time. Also, in order to remain sober, the recovering person must cut ties with drinking or drug-using friends. Such severance cannot be faced without pain.

A wrenching change in life patterns occurs when the chemical itself is removed from the alcoholic's or addict's life. This is a loss — as if the most intimate friend or lover has gone away or died. For a long and intense period of time, the focus of the chemically dependent person's very existence has been the drug, and now that "primary relationship" has dissolved. Gone, too, are the patterns of stealthy behavior, deception, and craft which — in spite of the pain they caused to self and others — added a certain challenge and adventure to life.

Though the elation of newly found sobriety may sustain the recovering person through the process of change, there are bound to be feelings of emptiness, certain gaps in experience, times when old ways have not yet been replaced with clearly embraced new ways. The void appears threatening. New ways of feeling secure and safe will come in time; new relationships will develop. But loss lingers below the joy of new freedom during the awkward period of transition.

The sick self, once seemingly secure in patterns of dependency, deserves to be grieved for by the recovering person, who is now in the process of giving up unhealthy securities for new, healthy ones. The recovering person no longer can take refuge in the label, "invalid," so often applied to the physically and emotionally deteriorating alcoholic (although neither dependency nor other kinds of illness can render a human being *invalid* as a person!). With sobriety and positive change, the person *feels* that his or her validity as a human being is beginning to be restored. Recovery means giving up the safe illusion of having resigned from the human race. But happily, it also means developing a new sense of belonging, as fear and denial are broken through.

Since chemical dependency is a family disease, a disease of human systems, others close to the chemically dependent person will also experience certain grievous losses. During the active phase of the disease, those in the family may have lost a sense of integrity as important, secure and cared-for members of a family unit. Each person copes with this loss in a different way, usually by assuming a workable role.

In his book, *If Only My Family Understood Me ...*, Don Wegscheider describes predictable roles which family members take on during times of emotional disintegration and stress. In the case of chemical dependency, the alcoholic or drug-dependent person is identified as the Victim. The Protector assumes the major responsibility for keeping the family in balance and shielding the Victim. The Caretaker becomes the family servant, busily and sometimes frantically looking out for the others. The Forgotten Child or Lost Child is often a middle child who withdraws into a world of fantasy.

The Family Pet plays the clown to distract the family — and everyone else — from the family's troubles. The Problem Child acts out feelings of hurt and rejection and establishes the reputation of troublemaker. Someone outside the family often completes the picture of systemic disease by playing the role of Professional Enabler, that is, a counselor or therapist who becomes entangled in the problem. This person may lack insight into the true nature of the disease or may be deriving a sense of self-worth from the involvement with the family.

All of these roles are created in reaction to a crisis, — in this case, one person's chemical dependency — and the resulting emotional turmoil and desolation. When the Victim becomes free and responsible, these other roles are affected. Each family member must look for new and more authentic ways of establishing an identity. This involves a disconnection from the past, from a system which — no matter how unhealthy — worked within its own terms. The burden of change is perhaps greatest for the one closest to the Victim, the chief enabler, usually the Protector spouse. This family member has been the most controlled by the disease, and as a result has become the most controlling. She or he has to give up control. This is the most confusing and grievous loss for a co-dependent person whose identity and self-worth have been more and more tied up in the role of Protector. Self-worth — and merely locating one's Self — must come in new ways, separate from the old role.

Family members may feel a psychological impact similar to that reported by certain World War II concentration camp inmates who, when peace was declared, were seen to wander into the light and become terrified by the unfamiliar freedom of movement which met them. They turned and walked back in the direction of the dark which had confined, tortured, and yet protected them from the responsibilities of the world for so long. They needed time to move out into the light and not be afraid. In a sense, they needed to grieve over the loss of the perverse "benefits" of imprisonment.

The hurts of recovery heal by reconnecting the estranged and alien parts of the fractured individual, restoring a person to the human family. Some have described this as "getting one's soul out of hock." The positive losses of recovery, which obviously far outweigh the troubling ones, are like the casting aside of too-heavy ballast that burdens the soul and causes one to sink. One grows lighter from such loss, but one also needs courage for it, for rising to the light, to fresh air, to the breath of new being.

Continue Becoming the Person You Want to Be

The future is like death —
Unknown —
and requires as much faith.

So Becoming
is like Dying.

The lapse between
a single
inbreath/outbreath

a slash or question
mark in time,
the act of transformation

the monarch butterfly knows.
It flies alone.

Sometimes the dead do not know they have died.
Sometimes the winged one dreams itself a cocoon.

Everlasting Change comes, all the same.

Nine

Separation

Late Contingence

If we meet again in life what has
passed will remain as we, greeting,
Farewell in the Compline of our days.

We shall look and pass as life has
always caused us to pass, and smile
and then backstep to our faces

where I shall read a tale of undaunted
hope in the pages of your brow,
and in my eyes the lines of memory will betray me.

And you shall heave a sigh without
Goodbye, but Godspeed until next
we pass — and I shall nod,

and all things remain as we.

Parting: Separation

Saying goodbye to someone you love. Leaving. Letting
go. Does anyone ever do it well? There is pain in
physical separation from loved ones. A vital part of
you holds onto a place inside the loved one; part of
you is still with you, part of you with the one you love.
But always you are aware of not being together, not

being in one place with yourself, being separated inside your own being — here and not here.

Parting happens because life requires it, circumstances necessitate it, even though the heart doesn't want it. Parting happens because of a need to work, to travel, to study, to move.

It is never easy to be away — from a spouse, a lover, from friends and family, from a beloved and needed place. My own heart will never cease to crave the mountains of the Pacific Northwest, which I left ten years ago in order to work and study in the flat middle of the country. Does one ever get used to it — living with this craving? With me, it is almost a physical need. After ten months, my blood begins to curdle. I know immediately what is wrong; I need a "fix" of the mountains. I need the sight and smell of a high evergreen forest with a snow-covered volcano cascading across the sky. I need the wild ocean and the pure lakes of the high West Coast. Vacation time comes, and off I go. At my first sight of the mountains from a car or plane everything is all right again — my blood smooths, the muscles and nerves grow calm. I live in the shadow of the great white mountains for a few weeks and am completely restored. That is a strong physical and spiritual bond which I do not ever want to break. Yes, I admit I'm addicted. I do not ever want to be weaned from those mountains that to me mean home and safety, majesty and challenge.

Of course, I need the friends whom I also love and left behind. I only hope I do not offend my human loved ones by carrying on so about the mountains — I'll not say which is more important! I only know that

when I am away too long from either the intimate friends of my past, or the land which shaped me, I grieve. And nothing will heal me but to return. This means I must have innumerable partings and reunions. The pain of each parting is only made bearable by anticipation of the next joyous reunion.

When love exists, the bond which transcends physical separation makes any parting only partial. Love unites across time and miles. We have all had the experience of being with someone whom we haven't seen for a long time and picking up the relationship exactly where we left it with each other. Each relationship lives on its own terms and takes its own time. Even when two people have changed, or one has changed more dramatically than the other, the relationship is almost like a third entity that contains the other two and rubs them together until they once again fit each other. That is the magic that happens when deep love and caring exist between two people, no matter how much has happened to them separately. The assurance of this, in spite of occasional fears and doubts, makes it possible for us to be away from loved ones, confident in the joy of an enriching reunion. When no reunion is in sight, the pain of being deprived of this promise can be very great. Yet, if the bond is real, the loved one from whom I am physically separated for a time or forever will always live inside me and be with me, just as the ocean I love is in my blood, and an image of the beautiful white mountains I love rests like a triangular jewel over my heart. Much harder to bear is the actual death of the relationship, the breaking of the bond.

Divorce: Dissolution

The legal term for divorce these days is "dissolution." A marriage ends because a relationship dissolves. When something dissolves it disappears. We know that any bond can be dissolved, not only one between spouses, but between friends or other kinds of related people as well. An emotional and physical severance. A cutting off. So much more than physical presence is lost when a relationship dissolves, when spouses or friends or parents and children or entire families are "divorced" from each other.

People must let go of so much that went into the relationship — the security, the dependency, the need that kept the relationship going. Sometimes one needs to give up a neurosis that defined a destructive relationship; give up the games that imprisoned people in a mutually destructive trap; give up the thrill of the war, which may have been the only way two people knew they were alive together. Someone may have to give up being a child; lose the relationship that permitted him to be a petulant little boy, or allowed her to be a coddled and protected little girl. Let go of playing "mommy" or "daddy" to someone who needs to be released into the adult world of genuine responsibility.

Not only the family structure and the old roles must be left behind. Often a divorce or even a separation leads to the loss of friends who cannot adjust to the reality of two individuals, who know how to relate socially only to the entity known as *a couple*. Sometimes one or both former partners must find a new church, a new house, new clubs, a new neighborhood, and perhaps new schools for the children. There are many more things than each other to let go of.

Even through all the entangled feelings and confusing emotional contradictions that are part of the letting go, some attachment doubtless remains, some unwillingness to lose so much, some rejection of the deep grief of giving all this up. This may be sentimental or false, but it can still be painful when two people have shared great intimacy even if that intimacy was mostly destructive. Nothing is ever all bad, just as nothing is ever all good, and giving up the good with the bad can hurt.

> I went downtown today.
> Seemed like you were right there,
> us holding hands as always,
> walking down the street, laughing.
>
> But when I walked by all the store windows
> there was only one reflection,
> and I wondered if you ever hurt
> when you look at a store window
> and don't see me.

To be able to let someone go with grace is a tremendous gift. To face the reality that a bond has dissolved and no longer exists on terms that hold people together or make them whole. The most redeeming thing that can happen when a relationship dies is for the two survivors to wish one another well in parting. Sometimes the dissolution precedes separation, and sometimes it follows. Whichever comes first, the key to a graceful and gracious parting lies in the parting attitude.

Dialogue toward Parting

Let us not clash now.
Let us not kiss now.
Let us not caress
or quarrel or carry on
as friends and lovers do.
The time has come
only to gaze.

Let us drink a toast
of commitment each to each,
then let eyes locked
remain transfigured
as we go quickly.

Physical Separation and Spiritual Alienation

To be separated physically from something or someone is to have a physical distance come between, a space that keeps you apart. Though you may be apart from one another, you may still remain a part of each other. In spiritual alienation, you become strangers. The spiritual bond that can so often transcend physical space is broken and dissolved. This can feel terrible — to be banished from the life of someone, to be made to feel *other*, hopelessly severed and strange. It is possible to be physically separated from someone, and spiritually united with her or him at the same time. It is also possible to be physically near someone and feel the chasms that keep you emotional strangers. Spiritual alienation is much more than separation. The link which bound together your *essences*, your very beings, has disappeared.

Instances of Alienation: Violation

Violations of any kind have an alienating effect. To be a victim of a crime, even if only one's property has been damaged or taken, is to be made to feel alien and strange in one's own being. A private and sacred space has been invaded and contaminated while one is rendered helpless and immobile. The illusion of invulnerability and immortality is threatened or destroyed; personal power is defeated.

Worse yet if a trust has been broken, and the violation involves some sort of personal betrayal. Impersonal invasions are also maddening and outrageous. The elements can intrude; one's life can be diminished if fire, wind, or flood destroys what once was a safe space harboring familiar possessions that expressed their owner's personality and identity. We may be harassed on the street, or in the sanctuary of our homes through the intrusive instrument of the telephone. We may be deprived of human rights by an autocratic government or an abusive bureaucrat.

Then there are emotional causes of alienation: envy and jealousy, which divide friends and make lovers feel suspicious of each other; possessiveness that squeezes the freedom and life out of the one possessed; misunderstanding allowed to metastasize; malicious gossip.

All of these are small replicas of one form or another of rape. To be raped is to be treated like a contemptible object, to be rendered impersonal and powerless, to be invaded in one's most private being.

Physical rape is to be brought to the most grievous alienation of all, denied the basic recognition which one human being owes any other. The philosopher Gabriel Marcel has defined rape as "the substitution of one's own rhythm for the rhythm of another." Psychologist Rollo May says the rapist feels powerless and tries to regain power by taking away another person's power. A rapist is a violator who has lost a sense of belonging in the human community and seeks to destroy that sense in those made into victims. It is like the right hand trying to kill the left hand.

A rape victim has to work hard to reclaim a proud sense of place in the human community. Such a profound violation can touch deeply hidden areas of formerly unresolved grief. While working through the rage over having been raped, one woman in her forties was surprised to find that in her confusion of terror and outrage, the keen sorrow she was feeling for her loss of sexual choice and privacy opened onto another sorrow — the sorrow over her mother's death when she was an infant. In the midst of her grief over being raped, she confronted the unresolved grief she had never permitted herself to experience fully — having lost the comfort and safety of a maternal presence so many years earlier in her mother's death.

Grievous Alienation from God

We've already touched on one natural reaction in grievous loss — that of being angry at God, blaming

God for permitting us to suffer, permitting the illness or death of a loved one. This anger is not necessarily alienating if a person pursues it. Anger is a form of communication. Its natural direction is outward. Hostility is introverted and blocks communication. Hostility is a frozen attitude of alienation. Raging against God can be healthy, a form of showing a depth of feeling and caring, an openness to the possibility for reconciliation. The passive reaction of clamming up in one's soul is much more damaging to a person of faith. Loss of faith, loss of trust in the presence of God, is a devastating loss for one whose life has been shaped by belief. If one has lived by this faith, losing it can be a kind of loss of life. The extreme example of such despair is heard in the anguished words of Christ on the cross — the overwhelming alienation of those desolate words, "My God, my God, why have you forsaken me?" Yet, in expressing the despair, Christ must have found his way back to a feeling of union with God, given his last words, "Into your hands I commend my spirit. It is finished." A better translation of those Aramaic words would be "It is accomplished." A timeless moment of reconciliation.

Grievous Alienation from Self

Loss of self-respect for any reason. Loss of moral integrity through the violation of one's own conscience. Loss of physical integrity in injury or illness. Loss of intellectual integrity through any kind of mental disintegration in trauma or senility. Loss of identity. Feeling robbed of individuality, as a twin whose sister determined the identity of *both* women, without a space for two distinct people to emerge. Being made to feel *other* within one's own self (a stranger lives inside me). I am a foreigner in my own body. The ultimate self-alienation is loss of sanity, losing one's own reality altogether, a sickness of the soul.

Needed: the courage to work one's way back up out of the morass; discovery of a way home to one's self; hanging on; healing and creativity; finding an outer container for one's pain; or decision and action in making an appropriate container.

Syzygy*

I will try to draw my pain,
paint this precise suffering
into some moving figure,
a boat on water gliding
round and around the buoy
out of sight.
　　Trying to paint my pain
　　on a pattern of sunlight,
design burned into the skin
by fire — not of the spirit —
fleshpain.

The Janus hell
double bondage
(Will No One Unbind Us?)
Migraine.

*Syzygy: the relationship of a heavenly body, especially the moon, to the sun — in such a way that it can be viewed as either in conjunction or opposition, harmony or conflict. The state of seeming in intense opposition and intense unity at the same time.

What good is a pain?
Why is a pain to be cherished?

    Anathema
      Outcast

Outside on the green stage
immovable, Mary the Virgin
wears a cold cloak of gilt.

    In night sleep is an incident,
    victory of the essential nightmare
    riding me, filling the bedroom, indecent.
    Eclipse. Cyclops. Scream. Claws.
    Women blown to bits by shotguns
    concealed in satin.
    Women — I, a woman — eating their own
       intestines.

Ritual of blood.
Sacrament of the bullring.
    Victim/Killer
    embracing the cold
    glass woman
    in mythic death
    at zero.

      The circle of inner nothing
        (Depravity drive me, Grace revive me)

Blood lust.
I am lost
in inner space,
too fragile, bloody, fully.
My life in an eggshell.

Ten

Sickness

Recovery: Dissociation of Sensibility

A kind of fading,
procession of bones
disengaged from their
true-bodied selves
marching across winter
like vampired orphans
without sight or speech.

A kind of loss of self,
of unnamed substances
in the blood,
a bandaged blur,
a muffle of color
where eyes were,
no pearls but wide-staring
mummy-like spaces for non-seeing,
a lifeless lucidity.

Coming back
from this hollow time
Lazarus-like,
the soul knows itself
bound to the body fast
in an act of love
past time, piercing
realities in a shaft
of light.

Not before or after,
not youth or age,
not living or dying,
not the rapid clarity of heaven
or the slow slurred speech of earth:
none of these is truth,
but the confusion of the in-between.

In sickness, alienation from one's own body occurs. The body seems to be alienated even from itself. There is the feeling of being no longer at home inside oneself. The skin hangs loosely over the soul.

Self-image and Sickness

In physical illness the appearance changes. The color is different — pale or flushed, yellow or grey. The eyes lack luster or have too much luster. The skin is softer or tougher. The body moves differently. A stranger has moved in, and I am no longer myself or at ease with myself. I know the psychological insult of being invaded by a *dis-ease* or a wound, the insult of being objectified into a *patient*, as if that noun had taken on the full meaning of the adjective. *Patient* is *how I must act* not *what I am*. Although I must be patient for my own healing, I also must be an *active agent* of my own healing, not a passive patient being healed by technicians and strangers. They are only my necessary helpers. I am my own healer, by the grace and power of God within me. That I must remember.

If I face the removal of a part of my body in surgery, I need time to say goodbye to that part of me: if a breast, I need to thank that part of my body for beauty and nurture, for being a source of pleasure and joy to me, perhaps a way of communicating with a lover or with a child; if a uterus, I need to thank my womb for giving me the possibility or the actuality of being a life-bearer, and for showing me each month the mystery of fullness, loss, and recovery, for teaching me life's and my own rhythms. If an eye must be removed, I can explore the gift of vision and again express gratitude, preparing myself for the refinement of inner vision and the tuning of other senses to compensate for the eye's gift. The expression of gratitude is always a graceful way to say goodbye, even to a part of ourselves: "I bless you, I release you."

If an organ such as a gall bladder is to be removed, I can learn the function of that organ in my physical life, express gratitude for that function, and prepare to release the diseased part of my body.

If I have abused some part of my body which must be removed as a consequence, it seems appropriate to express an apology to that part — to a lung contaminated by smoking, or a finger irreparably damaged through neglect of an infection.

If one understands how the body sometimes suffers for the soul in an integral psychosomatic bond, illnesses such as ulcers and colitis, which can be quite serious, may be treated from a spiritual as well as a physical approach in a special way: I may say to my stomach, "I am sorry that I have burdened you with my cares and anxieties, my anger and fear — all my unexpressed feelings which you have taken in to express for me. I am now willing to take emotional and spiritual responsibility for these feelings, to express them in some safe and direct ways, to relieve and release you of this harmful burden. I thank you for what you have done in helping me to bear my emotional burdens when I did not know how to deal with them, and I thank you for teaching me that I must learn to deal with them in a better, more direct, and healthier way."

Sorrow and grief are expressed by the loss of health to these organs affected by our emotions, and gratitude gives grace anew to the integrity of the body and soul functioning as one. The question, "What does this illness, loss, or pain have to teach me?" forms the beginning of a healthy resolution.

Illness of a Loved One

Or perhaps it is a loved one who is ill. How can I recognize the beloved features, the attractive vitality beneath the membrane of illness that covers my friend like a cloud, or a shroud? Something has come between us. Reality changes. Life slows down or speeds up. Distance shrinks or stretches. People blur. I imagine and share my loved one's longings. There is a craving to be touched or to touch with healing, to feel good, to be oneself again; yet a touch is felt as pain or not at all. There is a wish not to be lost anymore, not to feel helpless and hopeless, not to be a victim. To feel in control, in charge, having power in one's own life once more. To be useful. To enjoy oneself. To be as before.

Illness and injury are insulting to the organism. Impersonal, arbitrary, they attack and they dominate. They have the power to shatter the self-image of the victim, who no longer knows himself/herself as a well person and must suffer loss of abilities, loss of activities, loss of competence, loss of pride and self-sufficiency, loss of independence, *loss of being able to take things for granted.*

What of the living death of a lingering loved one? When my grandmother was seventy she lost both of her legs. Physicians told her family that she would never survive the surgery. But she did. She lived for eight more years, but she was never again herself. Before her surgery, she and I said goodbye. We had always been very close. We both sensed that things would not be the same, even if she survived. After the surgery, she was lost to herself, and to me. She grew more and more out of this world as the months and years went on. In the end all that remained was an occasional flash of personality that could express rage over the mutilation of her body. I did all my grieving for her long before she actually stopped breathing, for she had stopped fully living years before she died. We, her family, had to be reconciled to her not really being with us anymore. She was only partially and poorly with us, here and not here.

We had to learn to love her as a different person from the woman we all loved; we had to learn to be with her in a new way, appropriate to the changes she had undergone. We could not pretend that she no longer existed — she did, but radically *different* in soul and body from before. We had to change our whole way of relating to her, making a brand new relationship with her that was as valid and loving as before, only *different*. This meant dealing with our own rage over her situation, our own deep loss of her vibrant presence. We gradually came to accept lovingly her changes and her new presence. What was of utmost importance to all of us was that she should not be deprived of any love or dignity because of her changes. She was as worthy of respect as ever. The thought of patronizing her or pitying her was intolerable. What had to change was our whole expectation of what she should be for us. We had to see her in a new way, recognizing a new image that was reality. We had to redefine ourselves in relationship to her, and we had to come to a new understanding of "wholeness."

A New Idea of Wholeness

What is necessary in situations like this is to come up with an idea of wholeness that includes a lot of unwholeness. More and more I believe that a perfect universe is one which absorbs a great deal of imperfection. Completeness contains incompleteness. Wholeness contains a whole lot of unwholeness. How freeing it is to look on reality in this way. No more judgments or recriminations. No more false guilt over the inevitable.

No more self-hatred or blame over failure. Accepting what is and using it to become fuller, larger in one's being than before. Allowing oneself to be neither here nor there, but in between; allowing a loved one to be in between, too, and to learn from this.

In order to find our way in the endless variety of reality, we need to be easy and less demanding of ourselves and others, but never to stop accepting the challenges of change that call us into ever fuller lives, even through the apparent diminishment of life. We need to let go of rigidity, give up panic, renew our wonder at the changing miracle of creation. We need to recognize that integration includes disintegration, as life includes death, as health includes pain and loss. Our acceptance of imperfect reality is, after all, a reaffirmation of faith in existence itself, a basic trust in one's own part in it and in the many parts of each of us throughout our shared and separate lives.

Limenality*

To live at the edge
I said,
I do not choose
but have been chosen
by the threshold.
Here.
I teeter,
stressed
beyond tensiveness,
a wild animal,

blackshining
she-lion
or she-bear.
Here.

*The only way out is all the way in.
The only way past is through.*

Young, dying
as surely as age,
a ragged goat
or deer,
bloodblack hairs
standing on edge
all lightning charged.

Brinked.
Born out of fear.
The beast I am alive.

*State of being at the threshold, balanced
in between, on the edge of things.

I teeter,
steerless
beyond sane,

a she-lion
or bear,

my body a quiver,
a furrowing roar,

trusting the terror.

Eleven

Success

Freedom

Freedom is death,
being Absolute Possibility,
unbearable waiting
for the escape
into a new cage
where

freedom as death
will return,
reclaim us,
until we escape
into a new cage
until

freedom as life
lights us
and we can rise
wounded, but healed,
from our comforting chains.

What happens when we finally get what we want? What do we lose then? One of my favorite self-reminders is "Be careful what you pray for — you just might get it."

Loss of the Struggle or Loss of Ambition

So you've finally succeeded, reached all your goals. Why so dissatisfied? Aren't you ever content with attainment? The moment a victory is achieved, you seem to pass over the enjoyment of it, immediately greedy for more, more, always more! What a contrary character you are! Yet maybe this isn't so unusual or mystifying after all.

If my success meant the completion of a creative project — the birth of a book or a work of art, for instance, — I may experience a post-partum let-down. As we give up our many kinds of "children" to the world, we will miss the delight in being pregnant with our tasks or dreams, the vitality and excitement of the process of creation.

If the accomplishment was the result of a group effort, there was a certain camaraderie in the struggle, a delicious sense of conspiracy in getting to this goal. I shall miss it. I shall miss the special kind of support that friends and colleagues give one another in reaching a mutual goal. I shall miss the muscular feeling of stretching myself, lifting myself up to reach the high standards of my personal goals. I may even miss the luxury of feeling exhausted and sorry for myself sometimes. Now I'll have no excuse! Oh, I may still push myself to exhaustion in order to maintain the goal, but I can't very well feel sorry for myself in the process.

I shall miss what struggle teaches — that we have no right to take anything for granted, that anything worth putting oneself out for is valuable and cherishable, that anything really worthwhile costs something. I shall miss the awareness of my own strength for endurance and perseverance that struggle taught me.

Learning to let go of striving, of driving myself. Getting out of overdrive, settling into a normal pace, I shall grieve for my striving. Though I complained about it at the time, striving felt good. I can't deny that now. I will miss what a long-distance runner feels in the accomplishment of a day — every mile driven deep into each muscle, utter fatigue, pain, but profound satisfaction in the knowledge, "I can do it!" Do I have to give up running?

Maybe this particular race is over. I survived the marathon. I can show off my trophy: "See? This is what I did." If I can just hang on to the pleasure of that knowledge . . . But pleasure passes too quickly after the fact. Maybe I can start looking for another race to run . . .

Sacrificing Failure

I find it hard to believe that anyone actually fears success. How can a person be dedicated to a goal and fear it? But as I approach this goal, the realization of what it will mean to give up this happy run may slow me down a bit, as if to perpetuate the pleasure of the race.

Sooner or later, if I am serious about my goal, I shall have to surrender the luxury of stopping short, the luxury of failure. No more sabotaging my own best efforts. If I try to prolong the process by braking myself short of the line each time, I'll lose the joy of the race altogether. My goal will have lost its meaning. Am I willing to give up the game to win the prize? To sacrifice a comfortable pattern of defeat in order — finally — to get where I'm going? Am I willing to give up defining myself as a happy loser — or a sad loser who is happy in the closet of self-pity? Can I give up the suffering I've grown attached to?

One gets used to being unemployed, unhappy, unfulfilled. Those conditions seem easier than their opposites after a while. Being outrageously happy seems like so much work! But an awful lot of energy is used up — is not only used up, but wasted — in maintaining a level of failure, too. I don't have to deprive myself of success, of getting what I want, because it really *can* feel good to reach a goal. I'll just have to learn to find the same excitement and joy in a dream-come-true as I felt in a dream-coming-true. I don't have to forfeit the joy of success in order to maintain the joy of anticipation.

The High Cost of Winning

If the high cost of winning is the joy of the race, the high cost of losing is the joy of the goal. One chooses. The important thing to remember is that there are many races in life. Getting through one successfully is the best preparation for the next race, and the next goal.

Twelve

Essentials of the Art of Grieving

Two Houses

This is my grieving house.
Like the Moon Houses of my mothers.
I withdraw here into open space filled
with comfortable red light to be apart.

It is like crawling inside an egg.
It is like being a seed aware
of itself rotting in the ground
but not understanding the strange new
shoots sprouting from its sagging wounds.

When I am inside my grieving house
I paint myself red for protection.
I practice parthenogenesis:
I give birth to myself.

The long deep love labor
of a screaming belly,
a belly in the brain,
a belly in the soul,
permitting my body
to be broken
among earth's grave
bones.

I swim in inner sea water
though I do not know how to swim.

Come near only if you are willing
to dye your skin with your own blood
and lie with me face down on the ground.

Later, we shall move out
to join the feast
in our common house of healing.

Time itself doesn't heal. It only gives us room to free ourselves, and the opportunity to heal ourselves of past wounds. Time offers us the eternal present of possibility. We determine that possibility, through our decisions and actions. We decide to use time well. If we waste the gift of time and fail to incorporate past and future into the present moment which alone is truly ours, the old wounds may not close. A hurtful word may be as painfully present in memory as it was when originally inflicted, perhaps ten or sixty years ago.

Most of us are living through grief or grieving through life much of the time, for life is conditioned by small and significant daily losses. On the other side of grief we can discover the joy and gratitude that come with new and *re-newed* zest; for every loss creates a space where something new and wonderful may happen. The natural state of well-being involves both the grieving and the enjoying inherent in any moment of loss with its change and chance for renewal.

Everyone who lives suffers as well as enjoys, that is true. But not everyone learns to live more fully because of it. Suffering itself has no value; it is the use that one makes of suffering, through attitude and action, that can have value. Although suffering teaches nothing, I can decide to teach myself through suffering. I can teach myself to become more human and loving, more honest and powerful. Living through desperation and despair with courage and honesty can prepare us to be more understanding of and compassionate toward ourselves and others, more discerning of the difference between avoidable and unavoidable suffering, more determined to eradicate the former from our lives. Above all, through loss experiences we can teach ourselves a new kind of joy — one which is large enough to contain our pain and to transform it into a new kind of power, the power to make us whole.

If You Could Keep Your Heart in Wonder

Our love is
the unfolding
miracle

that expands
our joy
to include
our pain.

Another Kind of Grieving

Most of us believe that we can only miss what we have once known. This is not always true. Sometimes we can indeed long for something we've never had. This, too, is a kind of grief — not for something taken away, but for something needed and never given. It is almost as if we were born into this grief, which can never be healed unless the longing is fulfilled.

A friend of mine, a wonderful woman in her sixties, has shaped her entire philosophy and life of love out of the specific loneliness of the single life, her always unfulfilled longing for an intimate companion, her grief for the spouse or mate she never had. She feels a special love and empathic understanding for people who are widowed. Often I've heard her say, without any self-pity, but matter-of-factly and with compassion, "I've been a widow all my life." Her loving presence, her kindness, her generosity have all been shaped, in a way, by the grieving of her circumstances as one alone in life.

She is a person who has used her grieving well. She has transformed her pain of lonely longing outward into love toward others. She feels less lonely and more connected with people when she is loving and outgoing, and this makes her a blessing in the lives of her friends. She enjoys her job, her professional colleagues, her vast creativity, her many friends. She has found a way — *created* a way — to live constructively with longing. She has achieved a remarkable kind of wholeness in feeling herself half of an unrealized relationship. For her, outgoingness, interest in others, and creativity are essential sources of survival — and joy.

178

In a way, her experience is the grief of sameness. What she misses is the challenge toward change that a truly dynamic relationship offers. She misses this with a mate, but has created it for herself with others. She has reached out boldly and adopted other people to care for, who will also care for her. She has made a family for herself out of her friends and co-workers. She has created her own challenge for change and growth.

A single person may miss something she or he has never known but can recognize in others. We recognize something when we ourselves have the potential for it.

Such recognition and longing are not confined to single people. Married people often recognize in single people the potential for freedom and autonomy that they no longer have. The circumstances or the discipline and commitment involved in a chosen or accidental lifestyle demand that some potential goes unrealized. For a single person, it is the potential for intimate, permanent companionship with a mate; for a married person — even in the most open of marriages — it is the potential for physical and emotional independence which is to a certain degree lost.

Some people feel that they have been born into loss! People born in poverty, or into families which are emotionally impoverished. People born and soon orphaned or abandoned. People born without siblings. Each circumstance of deprivation is also an opportunity for learning, a challenge for creativity — but it can still hurt.

People confined in prisons, or in institutions of any kind for long periods of time, lose the reality of freedom, the possibility for change that is so essential to well-being for most of us. Confinement also can offer security and protection. When a person needs those, freedom may not be missed much. For others, the loss may be grievous. The monotony, predictability, and entrapping routine of imposed institutional confinement can break a person's spirit, unless one faces the challenge and creates newness for oneself despite external obstacles — like the Bird Man of Alcatraz, who became a brilliant ornithologist in his prison cell, and the Blues Man of Cook County Jail, who organized a jazz group on his cell block.

Creativity in the Face of Reality

Being able to face fully the reality of loss depends on a balance between personal integrity and creativity. Integrity looks at something and says "What is, is." Creativity looks at something and asks "What new thing can come from this?"

Integrity forces us to see things as they are. Creativity allows us to use what is for the raw material of what can be.

People who survive loss and come out of it with restored vigor do so because they are able to meet reality with a certain determination and a certain imagination. They create new skills for themselves to meet a new challenge. They grow themselves into new life. This doesn't sound easy, and it isn't. But it is possible. And when it happens, it's wonderful.

Feeling One's Feelings

Beside integrity and creativity, trust in oneself is essential in the art of grieving, as it is in the art of living.

Trust yourself. Trust your feelings. Own your feelings; recognize them as *your own*. Feel your feelings. They won't destroy you, because you can learn to express them safely and constructively with the reassuring help of others.

Care for yourself. In coping with grievous loss, make life as healing as possible for yourself. Surround yourself with comforting basics: food, bed, the security of an income, friends or family. If your own biological family is not supportive of you, you can adopt persons whom you trust to be a family for you, to give you the nourishing support you need, with the shared understanding that in time this support will be mutual, even if it can't be for now. Provide a nourishing environment for yourself. Avoid major changes that will uproot you emotionally from the safety and care of loved ones, or from a familiar place. Put major decisions on hold if you can. Rely on the security of the familiar until you are more healed. If the familiar is *not* nourishing, protective, or safe, make external changes which are somehow guaranteed by friendly presences.

Allow yourself to suffer your own healing process, to suffer your own meaning. You need to discover what the loss *means* to you, and what healing means as well. Let it take as long as it takes. The greater the loss, the longer your recovery will be. The more meaning whatever is lost had for you, or the more of yourself and your life or time you invested in it, the more meaning, the more of yourself, the more life and time will go into the healing.

Healing Wounds

Earlier I spoke of the importance of giving up the pain of loss when the time has come to do so. We tend, I think, to cling to the pain as a substitute for or as a connecting link to what we have lost. If I can't have you directly, I will have you in this pain, and I will keep the pain alive and hug it to myself as a way of hugging you. But this is a poor method, and unnecessary. Far better to let the pain go and keep the connection alive with happy memories.

Still, there are some wounds which do not heal fully ever in this life. After reassuring you again and again that healing is always possible, I must now clarify my meaning and say that healing is also complex and mysterious. Sometimes it can happen only through the mystery of the wound itself. So for some people, the wound stays open, perhaps just a little, throughout life, and becomes transformed into a source of power and grace, like the mythical wound of the Kingfisher, the Christ-figure whose always-bleeding wound paradoxically was both weakening and strengthening. It was weakening on the personal physical level, reminding the bearer of limitation and the need for humility and self-knowledge. And it was strengthening precisely because of this reminding function, the hard contact with reality that it gave, and the power and wisdom that come from that — the power and strength to be open and vulnerable.

This is altogether different from selfish clinging to pain for reasons of self-pity, masochism or to gain attention from others. This way of healing is not a chosen way, but a given way, and it is not displayed outwardly or used consciously, but kept as an inward mystery to be pondered. Those persons with such wounds are saving figures, and their presence in our midst is usually secret. They are given the grace and strength to bear their hard-given gift. They are often the quietly radiant ones. We need not emulate their woundedness which is between them and God, but we may benefit from and emulate their radiance, care, and gentle strength.

Reconciliation

There is a flowering crab tree in my backyard. Last fall, the small, hard, red fruit failed to fall off the tree as it and the leaves died. The light leaves fell according to plan, but the heavier fruit remained, dried up and useless, but stubbornly clinging to the branches through fall and into winter. I looked at the tree in February, the fruit visible under the heavy snow of Minnesota. I thought, "For all your tenacity, spring will come in a few months and you — last season's crabapples — will have no choice. You'll get pushed off those branches by the new shoots coming up from underneath." Sure enough. That's what happened. In April I watched that tenacious crab fruit get pushed off the tree by the irrepressible new shoots. Ultimately, life takes the place of death. Dead things get pushed away to make room for more life.

The tree taught me something. I am like that too. No matter how stubbornly I cling to my pain, refusing to let go of my actual loss — to give up my grief —

sooner or later, if I am to go on living at all, I will have to give it up. The life inside me will push it all away in its own natural and right time. Eventually the life inside me will prove to be more stubborn than the death.

In grieving, I embark on a journey through my own soul's seasons: fall, winter, then spring, finally summer once more. A journey through death and loss into renewal. Through grieving, I learn new value for the gift of life. I'm forced to take less for granted, to be more generous in communicating my gratitude for the life and love that surround me, more generous and spontaneous with praise words. Life is too short to withhold soul-nourishing compliments, to let deep love go unexpressed, to let people pass through our lives without telling them how much they mean to us. I need to let myself feel and express my growing gratitude for family, for friends, for health, for the healing resources within me.

In grieving I need to say what was left unsaid, and to let myself hear what was left unheard — anger, uncertainty, forgiveness, care, love. I know that with help I can complete what was left incomplete within myself. I know that I can find my own time and create my own way. I can learn to live creatively with a bruised or broken heart.

To all of you who are now grieving:

Take as long or as short a time as you need. Become an active agent of your own life again. Discover the art of possibility. The tools are your own creativity and faith. You have it all within you. You can do what you need to do to be healed.

I wish for you as I wish for myself the courage to continue to suffer your suffering and die your deaths in order to live your life more fully and enjoy your joys more completely.

In the Name of the Bee & the Bear & the Butterfly

In the beginning, Bee.
Bee of fertility, blessing of flowers,
high priest of pollination.
Bee of My Lady's dreaming,
dressing her eyes, ears, lips, and feet
with golden honey, feeding her
with goddess food for holy milking.

Bee, Bee, lighting on her lotus hands,
kissing her lovely toes with your silken lashes,
leaving streaks of bronze and gold,
powder from your feet on her blue mantle,
Bee, beloved pet, Angel Bee, beckoner,
messenger, bestower, wonder
of the Mother of God.

O Bee, holy Bee:
be with us and feed us
with high-potent sweetness
and when we grow dead
sting us alive.

In the beginning also, the Bear.
Great Mother Bear birthing us
in your own image, you teach us
the bearness of life, unbearable
breathtaking bearness of you.
We, in your likeness, learn to survive,
learn to suckle in your furry bosom,
learn to choose within the forest
food to make us grow, growling and humming,
into the fullness of your stature;
learn to labor hard, to fight when needed,
to care for and be cared for,
to rest deep and play well
with you and one another —
we your children,
we your fierce and foolish
tender cubs.

Bear, Bear, you give us teeth and claws
and make us strong with your vigor,
watch over us desiring our self-sufficiency
in healthy measure:
"Bear, I lose my way,
Bear, I fall entangled,
Bear, I feel afraid . . .
Food you give me of your self,
milk of your honey-feeding body,
berries colored of your blood.
Not only do I drink and chew —
often, with the teeth you gave me,
I bite you, God."

    O Bear, Great Bear,
    make us your pride and joy.

And of the Butterfly.
Born of life's ending,
promised from the beginning.
All the age-old cocooning,
all the enduring of unendurable happenings,
through long beginnings and endless middle
of our worm-shaped selves:
the unborn butterfly clinging to the bark
an ugly small worm of a thing made tight,
having no way of knowing, no way of telling
from the tree or sky hope of any change to come.

But by simply being
a good and faithful worm
allowing itself to die
surprise! breaks forth
the strangest bird
from its soft, odd-shaped egg,
from greygreen into gold,
orange, yellow, blue, vermillion,
amazing lightness and freedom
with singing wings most Christly,
slipping so lightly and so largely
into the membrane of our souls
through crevices only God can know,
filling all the soft cocoon stretching
spaces of our human hearts.

Butterfly, brave Butterfly,
down the wormlike days
of all our discouragement,
give us the courage to open,
to turn into the unimaginable,
take color, unfold, make music and fly!

Epilogue

Transition

I find myself
in the time
between selves.

Eight years have passed since I wrote these pages for you—eight years and many deaths and rebirths in your life and mine. Now I have something new to tell you. My husband died. Three short words, and it's taken me weeks to find the courage to say them to you. They sit on top of my heart like lead. He was thirty-seven and healthy and I loved him beyond words, and he loved me. And we still love each other, and learn to love more and more. But it is different. Everything is different now.

He left his body at a few minutes past nine in the morning on December ninth. It is May, my birth month, as I write to you. There are a few things I must tell you. Please do not make the assumption, "Aha, now she knows first hand what it's like." I knew before. The first words of this book promise that I knew. But I never told you about the largest griefs of my life, except to share some useful insight. This time I want to tell you specifically what happened to me.

No loss is like any other. Each has something unique to teach. I have to pass on everything I am learning, though it will never be possible to stay current. By the time you read this, I hope I will have learned considerably more. But I am doing my best for you and for myself now, in this moment.

Phil and I had been together for fifteen years. I first saw him as he was singing and playing his guitar for a worship service. His body was moving so fast with the music that my vision was of a radiant brown-bearded blur, and I did not see his features until the music stopped. His radiance persisted throughout our life together. His sparkle was contagious—it sparked some divine source of energy, trust, and joy deep inside those whose lives he touched, especially in me, whose life he touched most intimately.

Ours was in many ways a marriage of opposites. He was tall, I was small. He was extroverted, I was introverted. Our gift to each other was to teach the value of what each of us was least comfortable with. I taught Phil about solitude and silence; he taught me about celebration and the songs of nature. From the beginning, music was our common gift—his folk guitar, my classical piano. I danced and he sang. But he gave me courage to sing with him, and he joined me in the dance. We began as exuberant playmates, and we grew into true soulmates. It took each day of our fifteen years together for us to achieve true marriage. It took an immense commitment and faith, and a willingness to struggle many times past endurance.

Because of our differences in temperament and style there were many areas of each other's lives we did not fully share, and though we shared them with other friends, we were always secretly lonely for each other. Last summer we learned to let go of our longing, loneliness, and despair—and of our reticence. Paradoxically, we let each other go in a complete acceptance and release from expectation even as we spoke the most honest words of our hidden longings for each other. In that honesty and letting go, we suddenly found each other as though for the first time, face to face, as freed and freeing friends. Then the miracle of marriage began. Our last six months together were sheer celebration. We had broken through a kind of invisible finish line, and we eagerly reaped our reward. We knew we had earned it! We had done well throughout a long process that had often seemed too fragile to survive. Those last months were like an Arctic summer—all daylight, shimmering and breathtaking, and filled with gratitude. Delight dominated our days.

Then, after feeling tired from a slight cold for a week, Phil simply burst out of his body. Medical evidence revealed that his lungs were filled with many large and small blood clots. The assumption was that the virus related to his cold had suddenly taken a perverse course into his circulatory system and caused his blood to clot. There was no struggle or suffocation. He simply stopped breathing. And an hour of the best efforts from a caring and zealous medical team could not bring him back into his body. This sometimes happens, that a virus will run afoul and attack a vital organ or the blood, but it happens rarely to someone who is young and healthy.

Phil had spent his last year on a kind of intensive spiritual journey, a crash course in living fully, richly, deeply. I look on December ninth as his graduation day. His growth could no longer be contained in the schools of mortality. His spirit quite literally grew out of his body. All the same, I do not like it.

Life After Death

You're gone.
How can I go on?
One second at a time,
time after time,
still loving and loved,
across the bridge
of your going,
back into my life.
I know you are alive,
but am I?

For two months I simply wanted to go with him—not to die out of misery, but to share in the adventure. Gradually, I began to heed the call back to my own body of those who loved me and wanted me to stay in my body to love them back in ways the body allows. My being was still soulsore from other recent losses— among them, my father's sudden death three years ago.

My father had been ill for nearly twenty years, but in the last year of his life, with the help and encouragement of those closest to him, he went through a recovery process which gave him a degree of independence and pleasure he had not known for many years. To celebrate, he went alone on a tour in England and France, and made new friends. He came back overflowing with enthusiasm and joy in his travels. Because the airline company at the last moment rerouted his flight's stopover from Denver to Minneapolis, Phil and I shared an hour at the airport with him before he returned to his home in California. He showed us maps and told us stories. I had never seen him more alive, more happy. Two nights later he died in his sleep. I can say—and I hope that you will understand—that he died a well man. Having achieved life, he was ready for more life, so he also graduated into the larger realms. I talk to you this way not because I am religious, or a Christian, or a priest—though I happen to be at least the latter two things—but because I have gone with those I love through their death journeys, and have seen and heard and felt them so vividly and vitally in unexpected ways that it is no longer a question of faith for me, but of knowledge, of experience.

When I sat on my father's bed the afternoon after his death, I saw on his bedside table a copy of this book you are reading, with his eyeglasses beside it. I had sent him an advance copy, specially inscribed—for I had stolen "Life is Goodbye" from one of his own sermons, and added my own "Life is Hello." The book was released to the public the week of his death, and I know that since it was his custom to read a book clear through before sleep, his last act before he slept that night and awakened with God was to read this book. I felt kissed, in that knowledge. For Papa, I wrote:

All Souls' Day

> Under the desert full moon
> I carry your bones
> away from here.

Tomorrow under sun
I'll scatter them
under the fig tree
you planted
thirty years ago
in another state.

Papa, you lost
yourself, you grew
in misproportion,
your body became
your burden, without
shape, but too much
substance at the end.   .

It crushed your heart.

You hated what mirrors
told you of mortality,
despised your body's
gravity.

But you died
in your sleep,
blessed, and
your flesh
went peacefully
to fire

giving forth earth
within you, only ash
of the white volcano
you were, your bones
turned into sacred
seashells: carnelian,
rose, ivory, oceangreen—
honeycombs! Worlds within!

You are yourself again,
and after fire, Papa,
your bones are beautiful.

Phil (also, with Papa and me, a priest) preached at his memorial Eucharist. When Phil left—to be honest, I want to say what I feel: when Phil left *me*—next, I wrote for *him*:

Flight

*"What is happening
in the universe?"*

"People are dying."

"Why???"

*"In order to become
more intimate
with the universe."**

Dark December
just before
the Turning
when Earth faces
her light again—

You, my Love,
among those stones
flying through space
in singing
bliss-to-be-free—

you have died
from me.

   Only bodily.

You have become
a star, Beloved,
and I a bird
passed through flame
in your passing.

Your face now
a child's pure wonder,
you gaze actively
at the cosmic star
on top of the Tree of Life
for the first not-time,

your face a diamond
shot-through, suffused,
ashimmer with Light,
you sparkle being
into my void.

After tears I drink
your eternal de-light,
heart's Desire.

I reach for you,
Beloved,
the hands of my bodily
(my monster) grief
stretching, grasping
to hold you,
my fingers shudder,
shiver and pass through.

With these mortal hands
I cannot hold
your light.

Then the loud wingrush
of motion, a moving sun,
your warmth suffuses
me, suddenly,
and I become,
eternally in time,
your light,
a living crystal
of our love.

*Conversation between my friends, John and Christin Lore Weber.

Fallout

There in the clear photograph
you stand in your best vestments,
smiling at me on some wedding day,
my husbandpriest, my brother,
your face sparkling and safe.

The yellow sign on the brick
church wall beside you:
FALLOUT SHELTER

You were husband,
brother, mother,
and church to me,
my family.

You were my fallout shelter.
   Now under whose wings can I hide
      from the horror of your leaving?

197

"Where Are We Going?"

"Where are we going?"
you said.
"I don't know where
we're going and you do
and I don't like it."

Our London tour.
I had the maps.
I led, confident,
experienced, there before.

Now you're leading,
launched out on your own
tour of timeless space,
ahead of me in death,
and I do not know
the way
or where we are going,
and I do not like it.

Aurora Dance

The last time I saw you—
sunset, the day after
Thanksgiving we kissed
Goodbye at the airport
and I flew into the cold
night, saw the great sweep
of northern lights dimmed
by the full moon off
the airplane's wing.

You left your body
and mine the next week.
You were young but
you can't be any older
than dead.

I look for you now
in the night sky, Beloved,
a great swathe of smiling
light from the high north,
playing with the new moon,
making lunar rainbows.

I watch and wait,
half-blind, keeping time
with the butterflies
in my heart.

Now I want to tell you how this particular grief is unique. Never before had I known what I can only describe as a pure grief. I never considered the possibility of it. Now I am experiencing it. I do not mean pure as opposed to impure, but in its scientific sense— uncomplicated. It is not *simple,* as opposed to complex, but *pure,* as contrasted to complex. It pierces. It penetrates. Because this is the first truly complete relationship I have ever known, the loss of the physical and familiar expression of it is completely pure. Because, by virtue of an enormous commitment to work at our marriage, we came finally to a level of integrity in which we were concurrent with each moment and every moment was complete—*nothing loving or true was left unsaid or undone between us*—there is in my grief no anger, guilt, or fear. It is pure sadness, commensurate with the love between us. I know that such a thing is probably very rare, but I am amazed that it is possible, and that is the main thing that I have to tell you.

Almost inevitably you will experience some grievous loss in your life. I may even assume that you have already experienced such a loss and are feeling its effects, since you are engaged with this particular book. My wish for you is that, among your losses, you might know this rare sweetness. If you must suffer, may at least one of your instances of suffering be formed from a truly complete relationship. Because this pure grief reveals to me just the degree of fulfillment that Phil and I came to together. It reveals to me what is in fact the greatest blessing of my life—and I believe of his life also. The miracle and gift (within the horror of Phil's death as it touches me) teach me that it is possible to have a truly fulfilling and whole relationship with another human being.

Earlier in this book I said that in grief one's normal personality traits either become intensified and exaggerated, or one experiences the opposite of them. In any case, one is not oneself. Normalcy leaves, temporarily. My close friend who was widowed a few months earlier, is an introverted, intuitive, thinking, judge. She was thrown off course in grief by "living in her shadow" as an extroverted, sensate, feeling perceiver! I, on the other hand, became more intensely what I am: an introverted, intuitive, feeling perceiver. Understanding this helped us to accept—and encourage each other to accept—how vastly different our grieving styles were, when normally we had thought of ourselves as quite similar.

In November I was interviewed for an article dealing with the first six months of survival after being abandoned by a husband or lover. I was asked to compare the grief of emotional abandonment to that of the death of a spouse. I can put it much more succinctly now. Years ago I experienced radical emotional severance from someone I loved deeply. It caused in me a despair of the spirit which felt like a pervasive poison. The way to healing and redemption of the loss was through bodily hope. We were both still living in our bodies, so there remained the possibility for reconciliation and healing within the relationship, or at least within our individual selves. (In fact, both kinds of healing occurred over a long period of time and with a new definition of our love for each other and its expression.) Phil's death came to me like a bodily despair, a piercing penetration that shot right down through the core of my being, but did not pervade me. It did not deaden either my feelings or my other relationships. These became more alive because they were more sensitized. And the way toward redemption came through spiritual hope. By hope, I mean not wishful thinking, but intense desire based on conviction. Both losses were horrible in their own way. I cannot say that spiritual alienation is worse than physical separation through death. I used to think so, but no longer. They both hurt like hell.

My metaphors have expanded. In describing how Phil and I had so newly embraced our marriage as a brand new reality, I said that I felt like someone who stood at the edge of a swimming pool for a long time, unable either to dive in or leave, and then I made the decision and plunged, but in the slow-motion time of being in midair aiming toward a new marriage, someone drained the pool, and by the time I hit bottom, there was only concrete below me—and I was alone. Phil was no longer flying gracefully through the air with me.

In one of the hundred or so precognitive dreams I had for three years and nine months before his death, Phil and I were hiking in the mountains. Suddenly a large boulder was in our path. We stood on either side of it and Phil said, "I won't be able to go the rest of the way with you. I won't be able to complete this transformation with you." I respected these dreams without being tyrannized by them. They did not frighten me, though they burdened me, for I did not know whether to take them metaphorically or literally. So I did a little of each. I began to talk about our deaths and funerals with Phil, sharing with him my plans for my own funeral. After several years of these occasional conversations, Phil told me exactly what he wanted done with his body and his guitars should he precede me in death. That was the practical attention I gave to these dreams, and the spiritual attention was in the commitment we both had to healing whatever wounds were between us in the marriage, and being as honest and loving as possible with each other. The fact that all of that was true did not stop me from feeling as if I had been run over by a long train.

Sometimes even now the waves of grief come over me, and I am stuck in a spasm, unable to move from unbearable intensity into release. It is not pleasant. I imagine it is like the contractions of childbirth. I have compared it to being born, giving birth, and dying all at once. I am grateful that Phil doesn't have to go through this. At least I am glad to do it for both of us. It would kill me to see him in such pain. I know it hurts him now to see me in it, but I am open to his comfort, and that helps us both.

Once I said this grief was a "cosmic ouch," and the person I spoke to commented that it sounded as if I were being bitten, chewed up, and swallowed. That, too. But none of these metaphors is final. I can let them go, am glad to do so, as I sense changes in myself and the process of incorporation: making this reality part of me without being destroyed by it. I realize this means *re*incorporation, and I will have to work at it again and again for the rest of my life. I can only trust that the spaces between spasms will grow longer and the duration of the waves of grief both shorter and less intense.

Phil's mother, my mother-in-love, has taught me something. I used to assume, along with most people, that the death of a child was the most difficult grief to bear. Betty told me one day that she didn't register feeling or meaning when someone would say that to her, and she wondered what was wrong with her. Then she realized that Phil was no longer a child, though he remained her son, and that made the difference. He was a mature adult who had become her friend, her colleague, in some ways her teacher and mentor. She felt the loss deeply, agonizingly, but at those levels. So I learned that the loss of an adult child is felt quite differently from the loss of a young and dependent child. We must be more cautious in expressing our assumptions to those who grieve! Better to ask, if anything, than to tell them what they "must be feeling."

Another friend taught me something else. In those few awful moments of self-doubt I expressed my hope that Phil knew how much I loved him, and that I really had expressed it well and often enough. My friend said to me so wisely, "You must have faith in the past. All that you and Phil did together, all your growing and loving, really happened. It is all true." I think of faith as belonging to the future, the unknown. But it is equally true that we must believe what we know—we must have an enduring conviction with our knowledge, and let nothing rob us of trust in our own experience. Sometimes our perception or interpretation needs to be revised, but our experience holds and cannot be taken away. This, for me, was another instance of being absolutely startled by the obvious.

This same friend reminded me not to be concerned about my own pain or its intensity. "You have to accept your pain as part of your own mortality and humanity. As you so often say, no one is exempt here from the conditions of being born a creature. We all suffer and we all enjoy. Allow this in yourself fully. You are mortal. You will die out of your body and its pain in time, but your joy will prevail, as Phil's does now." Thank God for wise friends.

I am reminded that in grief everything is experimental. I have no way of knowing from one minute to the next what I will feel or need. I have to be humble and receptive enough to accept all the help that is offered me when it is appropriate, and to express my grateful refusal when it is not. I have never been able to receive love without loving back, but now the only way I can love back is by receiving—graciously and gratefully. I have nothing else to give. I have to trust that this is temporary, and that others genuinely want to help me and love me, and are glad when I let them.

My energy is unpredictable and may leave me without warning. Recovery from major surgery is generally smoother and faster than this—something hard to remember because my wounds don't show. I have to tell people when I am bleeding or in pain or too tired to talk or listen. If I don't attend to these inner goings-on, I become angry and resentful, which isn't fair, and is my body-and-soul's way of getting my attention and forcing me to shift gears—usually to slow down or stop what I'm doing.

I have said that I should have a big blue "W" sewn on my chest with an explanation below: "Please be patient. I am recently widowed and cannot remember, plan, or think." I have never been thrust so exclusively into the present as now. Now is all I have. I cannot risk expectation for the future, and the recent past is still too painful. So all I have to savor is in this moment. And I may not remember it in an hour! That's all right. That is the way it is right now. I have to believe those who read this book and assure me that "It won't last forever!" I have to believe it because I've done this all before, in different ways. Those on a first-time grief journey do not have the assurance of experience. At least I am spared those terrors.

I have rediscovered, painfully, that grief is not only physical but physiological. A physician reminded me that if I had a series of medical tests right now, nothing would be normal. Every system would be a little "off," certainly different from when I felt well and happy. She said, "It would be a good idea to burn up lots of calories to get rid of all the excess toxins you're probably carrying." I did all right physically for the first month—except for diarrhea and loss of appetite. For the first two weeks I woke up every morning at 7:46 and sobbed until 9:05—emotionally going through the period from when my body was telling me Phil awakened, until the time when he stopped breathing that last morning. This was terribly hard on me because normally I go to sleep at around 3:00 or 4:00 A.M. and awaken at 11:00. I had no resources for being torn apart so early in the day. Finally I prayed for it to stop, and it did. Until then, I made sure a friend was with me during that time, because I simply could not stop myself from cataclysmic wailing, and my body was barely able to endure it. A month or so later, I lifted a heavy typewriter when I was already stressed and tense, and it started a muscle spasm under my right shoulder blade, a longtime vulnerable spot. That in turn—because I ignored it and drove myself to finish a task—started a migraine headache which lasted for nine weeks. Finally, with the help of friends and on the advice of several professionals, I began a course of treatment which worked well for me: daily discipline in hatha yoga, which I combine with meditation and intercession (praying for others), weekly massage (it would be daily if I could afford it!); hugs and laying-on-of-hands from any appealing friend who offered; vitamins as needed; cold packs and hot soaks as needed; and nourishing but not too-rich food, and no food to which I have a sensitivity. With that regime I am keeping body and soul together, and for me, it is (temporarily) a fulltime job.

I cannot stress too much the importance of being touched. I need to be called back to earth, to my body, through my body, through the earth. The tender human touch is vital to me now (though there are grieving people and times in grief that are untouchable—one must ask before touching).

Just as necessary to me is the soul-massage which the mountains and ocean give me, the forests and rivers, the flowers in my garden, the green pastures, and the wonderful large animals who graze in them. When I do not see my neighbor cow, horse, and calf in my back pasture, I feel lonely. They are my family also. And they are my physicians. They are so good at being creatures—at being themselves—that by watching them I learn how to be myself again, how to be a good creature. When I feel utterly disoriented in time, space, and myself, the animals ground me and recall me to myself.

One afternoon while I was having a massage and doing emotional work to release memories and grief from my muscles, something most unusual happened. When my massage therapist stroked the sole of my left foot, I sat bolt upright, stiffened, and stopped breathing. Neither of us was afraid, but in a few seconds Nancy said, "Alla, please breathe." I answered, "I don't want to." But I knew I was supposed to, and I obeyed, with shrieking sobs that left me shaking and trembling all over for a long time. Nancy held me until I was quite finished. Apparently that was the center of where I carried the effects of Phil's death in my body. I called it my death spot. Each week I decided ahead of time whether I should have her avoid it as a sign of my respect for my own fragility and limitation, or whether I needed to have an intense release: I knew where to be touched to get it! That to me seemed rather poetic of the body: the left is symbolically the side of the emotions and intuition, perhaps because the right hemisphere of the brain usually governs those qualities, and it controls the left side of the body. So it was a kind of physical double entendre that my left sole *(soul)* should be the precise place for all this to be let loose upon the warm pressure of a caring human hand!

Though I agree with Susan Sontag that it is wrong to treat all physical illness as metaphor (see her book by that title, *Illness as Metaphor*), I must also acknowledge that there are times, particularly in emotional stress, when the body expresses the pain of the soul in graphic, imaginative, and poetic ways. My migraine, for instance, expressed what I felt to be a migraine in my soul. I was clearly divided: the spiritual part of my soul serene, even joyful in the adventure of the new relationship I was learning with Phil, spirit to spirit, as he taught me to fly with him in the mind and heart of God; the physical part of my soul no less outraged, seething in a distress of separateness. I was living in both realities at once, and there was no point of contact between them. The spastic knots in my shoulder said "I don't want to shoulder this burden—I want it NOT to have happened!" The body has its puns, also.

There are other kinds of symbolisms to deal with. Anniversaries are vulnerable areas which need preparation to be borne. They symbolize events from the past and are charged with meaning. On the anniversary of my trip to England a year ago this week with Phil, I cannot stop myself from reliving our experiences day by day, but I can choose to remember with gratitude instead of greed for more, and I can choose not to look at the photographs which I know would be too much right now. I have to learn everything all over again, because this is like being a newborn. Everything is a little chaotic, very uncertain, and uniformly confusing. I have to learn how to remember with pleasure, to bring the past into the present, instead of trying to go back to the past and grieve over its unrepeatable appearance. The fact is, I *can* repeat it every time I recall it with gratitude. I do have the power to place my focus not on greed for the repetition of life's gifts, but on gratitude for their infinitely repeatable presence in my mind.

Phil and I made love for the first time on Valentine's Day fifteen years ago. This February 14, I felt irresistibly sleepy at 6:00 P.M. I was alone anyway, so I gave in and went to bed. As soon as the light was out, I was overcome with tears. Soon I was on the floor, and realized that I had tried to shut out the memory of that day. By trying to avoid a painful memory, I denied myself its beautiful significance. So I let myself remember, but with gratitude for having been blessed with Phil as a lover, instead of anger that I would never feel his physical touch again. I can still feel the touch of his powerful love, whenever I am willing to open myself to it. I did not come through this all at once or alone that night. I had just enough energy to call a friend on the telephone, because I knew I was crying too hard again and needed help. Someone suggested keeping handy a list of phone numbers of all the good people who volunteered to be "day or night" telephone resources. That was an invaluable aid.

Next year on Valentine's Day I will plan ahead and take the advice of this book by creating a meaningful ritual to acknowledge and celebrate what the day means to me. I promise you, I take my own advice! So many people quoted *Life Is Goodbye/Life Is Hello*, to me that I decided to read it for myself. The person I was eight years ago had wisdom for me. I paid attention and remembered what I knew. I was also glad to see that someone had validated my experience by describing it in print! "Why, that's just what I was thinking this week," I said. I suppose I can tell you that this book has stood the test of time and life—and I tell you this as a reader myself.

I know I am slowly getting better. When I sink into some self-destructive thought or action, I see Phil in front of me like a natural birth coach. He not only encourages me to breathe, but he virtually yells at me to shift my focus. I obey. My commitment, whether I feel like it or not, want to or not, is to attend and obey. And every day the Holy One sends me guardian angels—special helpers. Someone to take me on errands, bring chocolate, give me flowers or a back rub. When I say "Thank you, Angel," the person may be startled, but I explain that an angel is simply a messenger from God, and the message is *I love you* whenever a kindness is offered or a truth told carefully.

Recently my physical symptoms moved to my skin— all sorts of bizarre eruptions, not related to anything. I call them "stress bumps." They last as hives or hard bumps or broken blood vessels, for a few hours or a few days. They drive me crazy. They itch and are noticeable. I can tolerate tragedy, but such irritating annoyances send me over the edge. My vanity is revealed to me, and that is humiliating: I can stand any pain so long as it doesn't show! But perhaps these "stress bumps" are an assurance of recovery, like the terrible itching under a cast when the healing of a broken limb is well under way. The message is that I am itching to move out of myself and on with my life. That is good. A few days ago I wrote:

Awakening

The mother bird beats
against the bathroom window
for days—disrupting my sleep—
three hours each morning, her body
a battering ram into the larger world
she confuses for my house, against
whose glass wall she last saw
her child alive.

She cannot save him
from more life,
either way.

I, too, throw my body against
the Crystal Door.
It is not my intent to kill myself,
but to follow the lover/mate
who preceded me into the realms
of light we call paradise.

What I learn from this
is that I am awakening.
It is again time
of the morning star,
and I return with spring
to the ancient sea nest,
place where the trees
were born.

Now I can hear the call
back to the body
of those who love me,
and yield myself
to their hands.

We are not ready to go.
We are not yet happy
and well enough for heaven.

But together we can learn
to love and laugh with power
enough to walk safely
even on fire.

As I write this it is one o'clock in the morning. "Swan Lake" is playing on the radio. A year ago Phil and I saw the ballet in the Royal Opera House in London. It was his first ballet, and he was enchanted. I wept. The lead male dancer and prima ballerina both received roses at the end. I could not leave behind the image of them floating into the mists, lovers reunited in those realms of light. I am not weeping now, but remembering with gratitude how fully we enjoyed that night and its beauty together. If I am faithful to the practice of gratitude, I will get well. I must tell you that though I know great pain, my days now are dominated by gratitude. This empowers me to do the work of recovery, to come back fully to my body and my life, the work of a literal . . .

Reincarnation

Twenty years ago I stood by
and watched my mother watch her
cousin's wife, the Russian woman,
cut up meat from a butchered cow.
Both women are dead now.

Not long after that,
one after the other,
they died.

From time to time I still
forget that, reach for
the telephone to call my mother,
invite the Russian woman to tea.

Later, they all left me.
Father, brother, husband, lover.
One after the other, one by one.
It's hard for me to remember.
I have to let the deaths out
of me like a child, open
my soul like a woman opening
her legs for delivery,
and then bear down.

I bear down hard
on all these deaths.
Each one is unique, it's true.
As no love is the same,
no loss is.

I have to let each one
out of me separately,
give each loss the scream
that belongs to its own
love's ecstasy.

If I succeed, one by one,
in letting go, in remembering
myself, I may again know
that dreamy sweetness,
the smells of love,
what life is, the feeling
of emergence from bliss.

Three weeks to the day before his death Phil came with
me to the annual conference of the Minnesota Coalition
for Terminal Care. I was to deliver a keynote address
on the spirituality of dying and death. My talk was
named for one of the poems in this book, "Dance for
Me When I Die: Death as a Relational Rite of Passage."
At the end I led a guided meditation, asking the five
hundred health care professionals to visualize something
or someone they were ready to let go of, bathe the
image in white light, and say the "Love Mantra for
Letting Go" out loud together. Phil had a tape recorder
on his lap, and recorded all of this. I next asked them
to allow the image to dissolve into a larger gold light.
Then all joined hands and sang "All Shall Be Well

Again," together.

Later Phil told me that what he let go of was his own expectation for himself to please everyone. In letting that go, he accepted himself fully as a gifted and limited human being. He was happy. The night after he died, I played the tape in order to hear his voice laughing and responding. I decided to be my own audience and be led by the meditation. I visualized Phil's body where he was last in it, on our green carpet. As I bathed the image in white light and began to say the "Love Mantra," Phil's taped voice said it with me: "I bless you, I release you. I set you free, I set me free. I let you be, I let me be." In that unexpected and wonderful way, we said Goodbye to his body together.

On Christmas night I heard these words from him, which I passed on to our family and close friends: "You have all the amazing grace you need to get through this and join me in the light. I'm right here with you all the way."

I asked, "How can you be with me always, and with our family and friends who love you, helping us all, *and* do your own growing into your new reality?"

The answer was this:

"You know how we are created in God's image and like God?"

"Yes."

"You know how God can be everywhere at once?"

"Yes."

"Well, you see?"

"Oh!"

So love really is the great unifying force that communicates across time and space and through the oneness of eternity, to quote another wise friend. We remain one family. Yes, I see. We are always with all those we love.

Chickadee Sacrament

"Always day eats the night."
She wrote from Canada, the soulfriend
I'd seen once twenty years ago.
I thought my day had been consumed
by night until she explained—
the words came to her in a dream
and meant the resurrection when
the night of mortal pain would end.

So my Beloved's day has come
and my night deepened.
He died, but he didn't,
because his day ate the night.
Only his darkness died,
which is why I no longer
can see him.

I hold my friend's letter by the window,
drink raspberry tea, watch hooded
chickadees on spring snow.

They Eucharist on bread
I offered back to earth
and them.

I give thanks also,
though thoroughly
orphaned yet not
alone.

I cannot enshrine
our transfigured times,
Beloved nor cling
to your Easter body,

but again and again,
even between my night
and your day, our loving
souls feast in once and
future communion.

I have a beautiful photograph of Phil sitting in an old tree stump in a rain forest, head thrown back, arms thrown open, drenched in dazzling sun, and his whole being hugging the light. That is the nearest image I can gather of what it's like for him now.

One day in January a friend gave me another photograph of Phil. It is the occasion of her daughter's wedding, and Phil is wearing gold and red vestments, walking solemnly down the aisle into the light. I call this his graduation picture. Standing behind him in the doorway under an EXIT sign waiting her turn is a lovely woman also dressed in red—Phil's favorite color, the color of energy and vitality. She is the bride's sister and best woman at the wedding, at whose own wedding Phil officiated several years earlier. In the picture she is pregnant. As Phil was dying on the morning of December ninth, she gave birth to a baby daughter named Alyssa. I believe that Phil and Alyssa passed each other, Phil saying "Hi, Baby! Have a good life," and she responding "Hi, Phil! Have a good eternity." Alyssa's grandmother brought me three red roses with the picture—one for Phil, one for Alyssa, and one for me. On Easter Eve, in bright sunlight in Phil's parish church, I baptized Alyssa and danced with her around the altar as Phil sang to her from a tape I have of his music. He was singing the Garden Song, and I blessed the new baby with water, air, earth, and fire. We welcomed her and gave her the gift of her name (which her parents did not know means "Little Alla," and Alla means *essence).* We are all one family.

Now it is two o'clock in the morning of Ascension Day, the feast on which I was born. It is my movable birthday. I shall celebrate it by going to the ocean. A few hours ago there was a *tsunami* warning—tidal waves, the aftershock of a major earthquake in an Alaskan island yesterday afternoon. But at midnight it was cancelled. I shall proceed with caution, but it is my intent to dance in the ocean later today, after I have slept.

I am back home in Oregon. When my father died, I used my inheritance to buy two acres and a house with Mt. Hood, the white volcano in whose shadow I was raised, in my back yard. I am so grateful to have this holy place to lean into now. With the love and beauty which surround me, I am "a rich woman." My gardener said that to me one day as he planted a weeping sequoia tree behind the rock fountain by the wild flowers as a Phil memorial tree given by friends. I know my wealth. It is a wealth I shall be able to take with me when my own destiny is fulfilled, and I am born out of the womb of time into the world of eternity which holds us all even now.

Journey

One way or another
more naked when we die
than at birth.
Emptied.

Unharnessed.
Unencumbered.
Untangled.
Allowed

for the journey
only as much
as will fit
into the hand
of God.

Loving the Body

I have lost my place.
My body has become
a foreign country.
I no longer know
its maps or rules.

What languages it speaks
are silent to me or
frighten me to silence
by their strangeness.

They seem harsh.
They come from nerve,
and grate.

Life Is Goodbye/Life Is Hello

Even muscle groans
under their sounds.
Skin erupts in the effort
of trying to understand.

I am dried out
from loss of tears.
And sometimes
there are screams.

I grow suddenly dizzy,
caught in the white-out
of an inner tundra storm.
Without focus I cannot tell
if I am going somewhere
or holding still.

I want to move freely
in this country and
live here again.
I want to respond well
to its voices and weathers,
learn its new laws.
I want to feel its welcome again.
I want to be unafraid and peaceful
and know that, after all,
I was born here.

I need an interpreter in my own skin.
Friend, help me to find and keep place here.
Be doctor or lover.
Hold me, and remind me how.

About the author

The Rev. Alla Renée Bozarth, Ph.D., was the first woman ordained as deacon in the Episcopal diocese of Oregon in 1971 and one of the first eleven women to be ordained as priests in the Episcopal church. The ordination, which created a stir in ecclesiastical circles and drew international attention, took place in Philadelphia in 1974. She prepared for ordination by reading for Orders at Seabury-Western Theological Seminary in Evanston, Illinois, while earning a Ph.D. in interpretation (speech and drama) from Northwestern University, where she also received her M.A. and B.S.S. degrees. As recipient of a fellowship, she was trained and certified in Gestalt Therapy at the Gestalt Training Center in San Diego. Currently, she practices, "spiritual midwifery"—guiding others to find emotional and spiritual health—as priest and psychotherapist at Wisdom House in Sandy, Oregon. Wisdom House with its small chapel is a center of serenity and creativity for friends, colleagues, and those she counsels.

Alla Renée Bozarth was born in 1947 in Portland, Oregon. Her father was an Episcopal priest. Her mother was an artist and writer who had immigrated from Russia as a young woman in 1929.

Brought up in the shadow of the Pacific Northwest's majestic mountains, transplanted for a time to Minneapolis in the flatlands of the Midwest, Dr. Bozarth has returned to her beloved mountains and now lives in Oregon in the shadow of Mt. Hood. Her husband, the Rev. Phil Bozarth-Campbell, died suddenly in December 1985 at the age of thirty-seven.

Dr. Bozarth has visited colleges and universities throughout the country as a guest lecturer. Her special subjects: spirituality and health; feminist theology; religion and the arts. She also performs her own poetry and gives dramatic and dance presentations for special occasions, utilizing her performing arts training.

Her prose works include *Womanpriest, A Personal Odyssey* (Paulist Press, 1978) and *The Word's Body* (University of Alabama Press, 1980). She has authored two volumes of poetry published by Wisdom House Press: *Gynergy* and *In the Name of the Bee & the Bear & the Butterfly*, which was illustrated by Minnesota artist Julia Barkley.

Sparrow Songs (St. Paul Press and Wisdom House Press) was co-authored with her father, the Rev. René Bozarth, who died suddenly in October 1982. *Sparrow Songs* is unique in that it is the only book of poetry by a father and daughter—both Episcopal priests.

A special poem, "Transfiguration," accompanied by Julia Barkley's paintings, *Dragons of Compassion For Grief Of the Soul*, was presented to the mayor of Hiroshima, Japan, and dedicated to the solidarity of all people for peace. The poem has been translated into Japanese and the poem and the paintings are the first works by non-Japanese women artists to be placed on permanent display in the Peace Memorial Garden in Hiroshima.

Helpful Resources

Written Resources

Abortion

The Ambivalence of Abortion, Linda Bird Francke, Random House, 1978. A thoroughly researched and personal illumination of the Yes and the No of the issue.

Afterlife

Life after Life, Raymond A. Moody, Jr., M.D., Bantam, 1976.
Reflections on Life after Life, Raymond A. Moody, Jr., M.D., Two Continents, 1977. A physician's observation of case history accounts of life out of the body during moments of cessation of heartbeat.

Aging

Aging: The Fulfillment of Life, Henri J. Nouwen et al, Doubleday and Co., 1976. A poetic and spiritual analysis of life, growth, and death.

It Takes a Long Time to Become Young, Garson Kanin, Doubleday and Co., 1978. Down-to-earth wisdom, humor, and sanity from this book make aging seem a difficult and delicious process.

Birth

Birth without Violence, Frederick Leboyer, Knopf, 1975. An exquisite step-by-step description of the peaceful initiation into life on earth that human birth *can* be.

Chemical Dependency

Consider the Alternative, Lee M. Silverstein, CompCare Publishers, 1977. This guidebook and personal testament to living and solving life's problems blends text with journal/workbook exercises. By a nationally known therapist and lecturer and a recovering alcoholic.

A Day at a Time, CompCare Publishers, 1976. A pocket-sized book of daily readings especially helpful for those working Twelve Step Programs.

If Only My Wife Could Drink like a Lady, Jack Nero, CompCare Publishers, 1982. The moving story of a one-in-ten marriage to survive a wife's alcoholism contains important information about Alcoholics Anonymous (AA), Al-Anon, treatment, and the family disease of chemical dependency.

I'll Quit Tomorrow, Vernon E. Johnson, Harper & Row, revised edition, 1981. A most important classic in the alcoholism field.

I'm Black & I'm Sober, Chaney Allen, CompCare Publishers, 1978. The first autobiography by a black woman recovering alcoholic, a minister's daughter, now a nationally known alcoholism lecturer.

Chemical Dependency and Youth

. . . But I Didn't Make Any Noise About It, Cindy Lewis-Steere, CompCare Publishers, 1980, pamphlet. A mother's story of her teenage son's drug dependency and of her family's search for wholeness and health.

I Never Saw the Sun Rise, Joan Donlan, CompCare Publishers, 1977. A 15-year-old's diary, the true story of her dependency on drugs and alcohol, her treatment and recovery, is enlightening and hopeful for parents and teens.

Kids and Drinking, Anne Snyder, CompCare Publishers, 1977. Illustrated stories based on real experiences of three child alcoholics, now recovering, give gradeschool children needed facts about alcohol and alcoholism. A starting point for adult-child discussions.

Young Alcoholics, Tom Alibrandi, CompCare Publishers, 1978. Practical help for the vast number of parents and community groups banding together to prevent alcoholism/chemical dependency in their young people.

Death

Death: The Final Stage of Growth, edited by Elisabeth Kubler-Ross, Prentice-Hall, 1975. As the title suggests, biological death is shown to be a meaningful part of biological life. Each person's life is given meaning by the sure event of her or his death.

Questions and Answers on Death and Dying, Elisabeth Kubler-Ross, Macmillan, 1974. The first thorough and important discussion of death by a gifted physician/psychotherapist who tells the moving stories of her clients in language that touches everyone's reality.

Death of a Child

The Bereaved Parent, Harriet Sarnoff, Crown, 1977. A personal story of pain and triumph of one family's loss.

The Private Worlds of Dying Children, Myra Bluebond-Langner, Princeton University Press, 1978.

Death of a Spouse

A Death of One's Own, Gerda Lerner, Harper & Row, 1978.

Widow, Lynn Caine, Bantam, 1975.

Diet and Weight Problems

Mom, How Come I'm Not Thin? by Bill and Enid Bluestein, CompCare Publishers, 1981. The sensitive story of an overweight child. For children aged 7 to 11 and parents.

The Only Diet There Is, Sondra Ray, Celestial Arts, 1981. The author shows that the fundamental attitudes toward one's body as a creation of God, and toward food as a gift, have more power to change our eating and living habits than any fad diet program. Respect and good stewardship of the gift are the miraculous keys to health and beauty.

Thin Is a State of Mind, Nancy Bryan, Ph.D., CompCare Publishers, 1982. A scholarly, complete work about how to lose weight by "not trying," by changing your ideas of self and the universe.

Divorce

Creative Divorce, Mel Krantzler, New American Library, 1975. Describes the emotional and practical phases of divorce.

226

The Divorce Experience, Morton Hunt and Bernice Hunt, McGraw-Hill, 1977. An in-depth exploration of the psychology of divorce.

The Boys and Girls Book About Divorce, Richard A. Gardner, Bantam, 1971. For parents and children meeting divorce together.

A Service of Affirmation When Parents Are Separating, a Forward Movement pamphlet, 1980. (See page 14 for address.)

Surviving the Breakup, Judith S. Wallerstein and Joan Berlin Kelly, Basic Books, 1980. Emphasis is on the lives of the children in studies of sixty families after divorce. Lucid, well-documented.

Dreams

Dream Makers: Discovering Your Breakthrough Dreams, Richard Corriere and Joseph Hart, Funk & Wagnalls, 1977. A clear and helpful instruction guide for working with one's dreams.

Dreams: A Way to Listen to God, Morton Kelsey, Paulist Press, 1978. A Jungian who is also an Episcopal priest speaks simply and theologically.

Living Your Dreams, Gayle Delaney, Harper & Row, 1979. A practicing psychologist and dream therapist describes how to interact consciously with one's dreams in exciting, effective ways, from a Jungian perspective.

Faith and Grief

Good Grief, Granger E. Westberg, Fortress Press, 1962. Pictures and a brief text evoke strong feelings of faith and expressive grieving.

A Grief Observed, C.S. Lewis, Seabury Press, 1961. Lewis describes his own grieving process, his anger at God, his doubt, and his finally deepening faith through the prolonged and painful process of his spouse's dying.

Family Crisis

If Only My Family Understood Me, Don Wegscheider, CompCare Publishers, 1979. How family members react to a crisis, including alcoholism/chemical dependency. Describes predictable family roles — Victim, Protector, Caretaker, Problem Child, Forgotten Child, Family Pet — as well as the Professional Enabler.

Grief and Disease

The Broken Heart: The Medical Consequences of Loneliness, James J. Lynch, Basic Books, 1977. A physician writes of the intricate relationship between emotional pain and physical illness.

Getting Well Again, O. Carl Simonton, Stephanie Matthews-Simonton, and James L. Creighton, Bantam, 1980. A physician and two psychotherapists describe a method for self-healing based on their work with people who have cancer.

Grieving and Children

How It Feels When a Parent Dies, Jill Krementz, Knopf, 1981. The stories of eighteen children, 7 to 16 years old, honestly told.

Learning to Say Goodbye When a Parent Dies, Eda LeShan, Macmillan, 1976. An understandable book for children in grades three through seven.

The Tenth Good Thing about Barney, Judith Viorst, Atheneum, 1971. A mother and father help their young son deal with the death of a loved cat by recalling the ten best things about him.

Healing

Anatomy of an Illness as Perceived by the Patient: Reflections on Healing and Regeneration, Norman Cousins, W.W. Norton, 1979. The author tells how he healed himself of a rare disease through the regenerative power of rest and laughter.

Healing and Wholeness, John A. Sanford, Paulist Press, 1977. The psychology and spirituality of healing, from a Jungian perspective.

Laugh after Laugh: The Healing Power of Humor, Raymond Moody, Headwaters Press, 1978.

Journal-keeping

One to One, Christina Baldwin, J.B. Lippincott, 1977. A working guide that is not overwhelming.

Loneliness

Lifelines, Lynn Caine, Doubleday, 1978. The author describes feelings of depression associated with a loss of the sense of self-worth and self-confidence, and demonstrates a survival system in dealing with the destructive elements of loneliness.

Loss of a Love

How to Survive the Loss of a Love, Colgrove et al, Simon & Schuster, 1976. Concise and practical suggestions for coping. Compact poems conclude each brief chapter with bull's eye accuracy.

Mastectomy

Three Weeks in Spring, Joan H. Parker and Robert B. Parker, Houghton Mifflin, 1978. A gutsy personal story told with honesty and compassion.

Mid-life Crisis

Passages, Gail Sheehy, Bantam, 1977. All of us can recognize ourselves in the phases of life described here as critical and change-making.

Parenting

Parenting, Samellyn Wood et al, Hart, 1978. Four different styles of life's most challenging task are explored.

Prayer

Prayerways, Louis M. Savary and Patricia Berne, Harper & Row, 1980. Integrative ways of praying with the imagination, healing meditation, and various concepts of prayer are described lucidly and usefully.

Pregnancy

A Baby? . . . Maybe, Elizabeth M. Whelan, M.D., Bobbs-Merrill, 1975. Pros and cons carefully considered in the choice to have a child. Best to read this before becoming pregnant, but it shouldn't give anyone regrets after the fact. It's helpful to have questions raised, facts clarified, or ambivalences expressed as soon as possible, but during pregnancy is as good a time as any for looking squarely at reality.

Rape

Against Our Will: Men, Women and Rape, Susan Brownmiller, Bantam, 1976. An epic work showing the cultural, historical, philosophical, psychological, physical, and emotional meanings of rape.

Retirement

The Retirement Book, Joan Adler, William Morrow & Co., 1975. Covers the spectrum of finances, housing, insurance, hobbies, skill-implementation, families, travel, work, romance, and health.

Ritual

"Ritual . . . as Communication and as State," Roy A. Rappaport, in *The Co-Evolutionary Quarterly*, Summer, 1975. Ritual is defined as "reconciliation in change," by this philosopher in a highly fascinating and intellectual exploration of ritual and society, art, religion, interpersonal communication, and the world of animals and grace.

Suffering

Disease, Pain, and Sacrifice: Toward a Psychology of Suffering, David Bakan, Beacon Press, 1971. Another philosopher writes in a highly condensed style, examining myth and meaning in connection with the human experience of suffering.

Visualization

Seeing with the Mind's Eye, Mike Samuels and Nancy Samuels, Random House, 1975.

Motion Pictures

Resurrection, starring Ellyn Burstyn, produced by Renée Missel and Howard Roseman, Universal Pictures, 1980.

Tell Me a Riddle, Godmother Productions, 1981, from a novella by Tillie Olson.

Other Resources

Check the yellow pages of the telephone directory in your city or the city nearest you for information on types of services available for your particular needs. Look under "Social Services" or "Marriage and Family Counseling" or "Alcoholism Information and Treatment Centers" for appropriate resources such as:

Grief centers
   Usually for the widowed and divorced, but anyone in any kind of grief may participate in support groups.
   Rape and crisis counseling centers

Crime victim counseling

Alcoholism/chemical dependency information and treatment

Comprehensive Care Corporation has over one hundred treatment centers, clinics, and information centers around the United States.

Transition counseling

For divorce and mid-life transitions.

We Care has support groups for divorced persons.

Disease counseling

I Can Cope and Make Every Day Count are support groups for people who have cancer. Contact the American Cancer Society.

Mastectomy counseling

Reach for Recovery offers help for women recovering from breast surgery.

Other kinds of spiritual, psychological, medical, career or parenthood counseling are available. Watch the newspapers for announcements or features about special programs. Seek professionals prepared to help.